Date Due

Jan 29 '69		
Mar 19 69		
PHS OCT		

CAT. NO 24 162   PRINTED IN U.S.A.   bd

FRANCES PERKINS:

First Lady of the Cabinet

by Don Lawson

FRANCES PERKINS

*First Lady
of the
Cabinet*

ILLUSTRATED WITH PHOTOGRAPHS

Abelard-Schuman
LONDON NEW YORK TORONTO

London	New York	Toronto
Abelard-Schuman	Abelard-Schuman	Abelard-Schuman
Limited	Limited	Canada Limited
8 King St. WC2	6 West 57th St.	896 Queen St. W.

Printed in the United States of America

BOOKS BY DON LAWSON
Famous American Political Families
Frances Perkins: First Lady of the Cabinet
The United States in the Korean War
The United States in World War I
The United States in World War II
The War of 1812: America's Second War for Independence
Young People in the White House

to
Frances Perkins,
one of the truly
great figures in
modern American
history, and
someone I very
much wish I could
have personally
known

CONTENTS

PHOTOGRAPHS

ACKNOWLEDGMENTS

Frances Perkins was extremely reticent regarding her private life. "I do not like personal publicity," she said. "I've always believed that a woman's job and her personal life should be completely separate." Miss Perkins went on to explain that she thought of her public life as a public trust, open to hard scrutiny and sharp criticism. "My private life, however, is strictly my own," she added.

I find this a refreshing and extremely admirable trait in a woman, particularly in a woman who was a public figure from the time she was a young lady right up to the day of her death. I must hasten to add, however, that such an attitude makes the role of a biographer an extremely difficult one indeed.

Valuable background material about the era in which Frances Perkins played such an important role will be found in the books listed in the bibliography at the end of this volume. But most of the vital biographical information about this great lady lies more or less buried in old and yellowing files of newspapers and magazines dating back to the turn of the century. The Chicago Public Library proved to be a tremendously valuable source for these old newspapers and magazines, many of whose names have been long forgotten. My tireless guide at the Chicago Public Library was Mrs. Roberta Sutton, chief of the Research Department. Truly, I would have been lost in tracking down biographical source material about Frances Perkins without Mrs. Sutton's vast research skills and great determination.

I also wish to acknowledge the invaluable assistance of Wayne M. Hartwell, librarian of the *Encyclopaedia Britannica,* as well as the assistance of Verne Pore, assistant to the editor-in-chief of *Compton's Pictured Encyclopedia.* Great thanks are also due to Bernie Holliday for his work on the photographs and to Eunice Mitchell, without whom the manuscript for this book would not have been typewritten.

Finally, I wish to thank the Viking Press, Inc., for granting me permission to use material from the following book:

> *The Roosevelt I Knew* by Frances Perkins
> Copyright 1946 by Frances Perkins
> Reprinted by permission of The Viking Press, Inc.

—DON LAWSON

*"Being a woman has only bothered me
in climbing trees."*

—Frances Perkins

1

FLASH FIRE!

On an afternoon in late March, 1911, a group of young ladies sat drinking tea and chatting in an elegant old drawing room overlooking New York City's Washington Square. Outside, there was a chill in the air. Inside, there was the warmth of the room itself as well as the warmth of friendship and talk and laughter.

Frances Perkins had been looking forward to this afternoon. She loved her job as a social worker, but it was an exhausting one. These brief hours with her friends always restored her energies. Today she was eager to bring her friends up to date on the progress she was making on her job.

"Let me tell you the latest about 'Big Tim'," she said.

All during this past winter she had been working with members of the New York State Legislature to try and get a bill passed to improve the hours and working conditions for employed women and children. In her role as a woman

17

lobbyist—a novelty at this time—Frances Perkins had been trying for months to gain the support of one of the most powerful political bosses of the day. This man was a loud-talking, cigar-smoking New York State senator named "Big Tim" Sullivan, who was also known as the "King of the Bowery."

"I think I've begun to gain his grudging respect," she said now. "Just this morning he paid me a real compliment—real for him, that is. 'You know, young lady,' he said, 'I like your ways. You can always tell when a man like me is lying, but you never tell me so to my face!'"

The ripple of laughter in the drawing room was cut short by the sound of shrieking fire sirens and clanging fire engine gongs from the Square outside.

Frances Perkins hurried to a window, drew back the curtains and looked out. Horse-drawn fire engines, hand-drawn hose carts and dozens of people were hurrying across Washington Square toward Washington Place where flames leaped into the March sky.

Her voice was filled with dismay. "There's a terrible fire in one of the wooden sweatshop buildings," she said. "All of the loft floors are aflame. We must go and help."

But there was little that Frances Perkins and her friends— or anyone else for that matter—could do. The flash fire had turned the ramshackle factory building into a raging inferno in less than three minutes, and disaster quickly followed for the scores of women workers who were trapped inside.

The eighth, ninth and tenth floors of the doomed building were occupied by the Triangle Shirtwaist Company. Near the tables on which the workers were making shirtwaists—

The Triangle Factory fire

apparel worn by all women of that day—were baskets filled
with scraps of organdy, lace, cotton and embroidery. It was
never learned how the fire started, but probably a match or
a lighted cigarette was thrown into one of these baskets of
material. In a moment the entire loft was aflame. By the
time the workers were aware of their danger, it was already
too late.

The fire escape almost instantly became too hot for use.
The elevator carried a few of the girls to safety but was soon
jammed with the bodies of women who jumped into the
shaft and onto the top of the car. A stairway leading to an
exit was filled with suffocating smoke and ended at a locked
door. Here more than fifty women died.

Outside the building the sidewalks soon became piled with
the bodies of women who jumped from the upper story
windows when they saw that neither the water from the fire
hoses nor rescue equipment could reach as high as the loft
floors.

Frances Perkins, a stricken look on her face, stood in the
street and watched helplessly. She saw one girl hang from
a window sill and drop only when the flames reached her
hands. Other girls waited until their clothes actually caught
fire before they jumped. Some covered their eyes with pieces
of cloth so they would not have to look at the certain death
that they and their friends faced on the pavement below.

Almost 150 workers—the majority of them girls and women
—lost their lives in the Triangle Factory fire. New York City
and the nation were shocked. Frances Perkins was determined, however, that people should be more than merely
shocked. They must be shocked into action. She knew from

Workroom of the Triangle Shirtwaist Company after the fire

—*Wide World Photo*

her experiences as a social worker that the public had long been uneasy about fire hazards and industrial accidents and bad working conditions in general. This tragedy, if it was to serve any purpose, must spark a drive to improve safety and working conditions for all wage earners, both men and women. The Triangle fire, she was convinced, could be a torch to light up the sky of industrial reform throughout the United States.

2

BEFORE THE FIRE

The Triangle Shirtwaist Factory fire took place just a few weeks before Frances Perkins' twenty-ninth birthday. The second daughter of Frederick W. and Susan Wright Perkins, Frances had been born on April 10, 1882, in Boston. Christened Frances Cora Perkins, she soon became known as "Fanny Cora" to her family and friends.

Fanny Cora's father was the co-founder of a twine manufacturing company. He was no ordinary businessman, however, but a classical scholar who loved to tell tales of Greek mythology to his little daughter at the dinner table. Although he and his wife were conservative Republicans, Mr. Perkins also liked to tell Fanny Cora stories about several of the family's early ancestors who were noted for their fierce independence and liberalism. She learned to be particularly proud of James Otis, a relative on her mother's side of the family, who had gained fame during Revolutionary War

23

days for denouncing the British for their treatment of the American colonists.

When Frances was still a young girl, she demonstrated her own independence by announcing to her staunchly Republican family that she was a Democrat. She had decided on her own that the Democrats were more interested than the Republicans in the welfare of the poor. She never afterwards changed her mind, despite a certain amount of disillusionment she later experienced in dealing with the practical politicians in her chosen party.

Although she was born in Boston, Fanny Cora grew up in Worcester, Massachusetts, where she was active in Sunday school and church work all during her girlhood. At Worcester Classical High School she was a good but not outstanding student. Nevertheless, she graduated at the age of sixteen, and entered Mount Holyoke College, where she majored in biology and chemistry. Some of Fanny Cora's fellow students thought she was too much of a talker—they called her "the loquacious linguist"—but she was generally popular and extremely loyal to her friends. She was something of a campus politician as well. During her junior year she was elected class vice-president. She also was chairman of the college Y.W.C.A. organization, and upon her graduation was elected permanent president of the class of 1902.

Frances seriously considered seeking a job as an analytical chemist after she was graduated from college, but her parents were opposed to women working at "men's jobs," so she remained at home in Worcester. She was by no means idle. She did social work for the Episcopal Church and studied independently. Her independent studies centered around the economics of social work, a subject in which she had first become interested in college. There she had made a survey of working conditions in factories near Mount Holyoke. Her observations during and after college convinced her that there was a great need for laws to protect young women and children workers who were virtually without any legal safeguards.

At the end of two years of social work and independent study in Worcester, Frances was offered a position teaching chemistry in a girls' school at Lake Forest, Illinois. She was delighted when her parents said they had no objections to her taking this kind of job.

Frances liked teaching, but social work also continued to have a strong appeal for her. On weekends and during school holidays she went into Chicago, which was just a few miles away. There she became acquainted with a social worker named Jane Addams, the head of Hull House. The welfare work for the poor that Miss Addams and her friends were doing at their Chicago settlement house seemed more worthwhile to Frances than anything she herself had done so far. She wanted to share in their efforts. At the end of a year in Lake Forest Frances quit teaching and went to work with Jane Addams at Hull House.

Jane Addams came from a wealthy family, but she had devoted most of her life to helping the poor. Born on September 6, 1860, at Cedarville, Illinois, Jane was just a little girl when she became aware of the hunger and misery suffered by poverty-stricken factory workers in nearby southern Illinois cities. She determined to do something about remedying the situation.

After graduating from Rockford College, Jane traveled abroad. Here too she saw people in the industrial centers of the great cities living and working under the worst possible conditions.

In England Jane visited the world's first settlement house, Toynbee Hall. She was greatly impressed with the welfare efforts of Oxford and Cambridge University graduates who lived and worked among the poor in London's East End slums. She decided the same kind of help could and should be given to poor city workers in the United States.

In 1889 Jane Addams and a close friend from her school days, Ellen Gates Starr, founded their settlement house in a run-down old mansion in the heart of the tenement and sweatshop district on Chicago's West Side. It was called Hull House after the mansion's original builder, Charles Hull.

When Frances Perkins began living there, Hull House was well along the way toward becoming the most famous settlement house and Jane Addams the most famous social worker in the nation. Some years later, in 1931, Miss Addams' work would result in her being awarded a Nobel prize.

Frances Perkins lived and worked at Hull House for six months. They were six months in which she definitely determined upon her life's work. Daily, she and the other social workers trudged through the neighborhood inspecting tenements and sweatshops. They were led by the crusading Jane Addams, who had had herself appointed to the job of city garbage inspector so she could demand that the dirty West Side streets be cleaned up. In the evenings Frances helped feed the hungry and nurse the sick who flocked to Hull

House for help. She also conducted evening classes at which immigrants of a half-dozen races were taught a wide variety of subjects.

Inspiring as this work was and as dedicated to it as she had become, Frances soon realized that she had not had enough formal training in the social sciences. She decided to leave Hull House and enroll in the department of economics at the University of Pennsylvania where she could study economics and sociology. In addition to her university classes she did social work for the Philadelphia Research and Protective Association, becoming that organization's executive secretary at a salary of forty dollars a month. She did so well in this job and in her studies that she was offered a fellowship by Columbia University in New York, where, in 1910, she received her Master's degree in social economics.

Soon after she received her M.A. degree from Columbia, Frances was named executive secretary of the New York Consumers' League. Her job was to investigate industrial conditions and fight for protective legislation for working women and children. In her role as a woman lobbyist, she frequently went to Albany where the New York Legislature met. There she became friendly with several politicians who, like Jane Addams, greatly influenced her career. One of these men was a future President, Franklin Delano Roosevelt, under whom Frances Perkins would one day become the first woman member of the United States Cabinet.

At this period in her career, however, Frances had her heart and head set on getting the New York State Legislature to pass a law limiting the work week for women and children to fifty-four hours. The man she had been trying to gain as an ally was a much more powerful politician than the newly elected state senator, Franklin D. Roosevelt. The man whose support she needed was Big Tim Sullivan, about whom Frances was telling her girl friends on the afternoon of the tragic fire near Washington Square.

3

SUCCESS AS A LOBBYIST

The public did not forget the Triangle fire. Shortly after the tragedy a huge rally was held in New York's Metropolitan Opera House. Frances Perkins was one of the rally's sponsors. It was both a memorial service and a protest meeting. One of the speakers was Rose Schneidermann, a woman who had been an industrial worker since she was a child.

"We cannot talk of forgiveness," she told the audience. "The blood of those dead workers calls to us all to prevent these things!"

The effect of Rose Schneidermann's words on the packed Opera House was electric.

"Those loft buildings were never intended to be used for factories," the speaker continued. "They were intended for storage and only storage. Even a simple fire drill shows at once how unsafe such buildings are. Exits are not large enough. What is called a fire escape is not a fire escape but a death trap."

29

In 1961 these women, survivors of the Triangle Factory fire, attended the fiftieth-anniversary ceremonies commemorating the tragedy in which scores of their friends and co-workers died

Seated on the platform from which Rose Schneidermann was speaking were a number of New York's most distinguished citizens, including several public officials. People in the audience now demanded that these men take action.

Rose Schneidermann began to talk about the victims of the Triangle fire. "Most of the girls who were killed had families who were dependent upon them. Those families may now become public dependents. One girl was working for money to go to college. She will never go. Two of the women whose daughters were killed are insane with grief. Some of the girls who escaped with their lives have been injured so badly they may have to spend years in the hospital. . . ."

There were other speakers besides Rose Schneidermann at this citizens' indignation meeting, but her words alone would have been enough. An organization called the New York Committee on Public Safety was soon formed, and Frances Perkins was named its secretary. She then went to work to get a bill creating a Factory Investigating Commission through the New York State Legislature.

Meanwhile, however, the fifty-four-hour work week bill was still hanging fire in the legislature. This meant that Frances had two pieces of major legislation for which she was lobbying. She had to spend most of her time in Albany, but it was time well spent, for she was rapidly gaining a sound working knowledge of state politics and politicians. She became a familiar figure in the hallways of the state capitol, and politicians and newspapermen began to ask who that little woman was in the smartly tailored suit and the three-cornered hat (called a *tricorne*). When these men talked with her they found her manner was frank and

engaging, and she spoke slowly and distinctly. She often
chuckled good-humoredly—one of the things that began to
win Big Tim Sullivan to her side—but when she was eager
to convince Sullivan or his colleagues of the justice of one
of her bills, her brilliant brown eyes flashed fire.

By the summer of 1911, Frances had won the complete
allegiance of Big Tim Sullivan. The young state senator,
Franklin D. Roosevelt, had also rallied to her side, and
Frances had come to regard him with increased respect.
When she had first become acquainted with Roosevelt he
had impressed her as an arrogant young man who had no
interest in the lot of the average working person. But he
had since shown a capacity to grow. Now he, like Frances,
seemed to have a genuine interest in the hopes, fears and
ambitions of the common man.

Toward the end of the legislative session, when Frances
had all but given up hope, the senate agreed to vote on a
somewhat modified version of her original fifty-four-hour
bill. The vote was bound to be close, so Frances went to see
Big Tim to make certain that he and his cousin, Senator
C. D. Sullivan, would vote for its passage. The two Sullivans
were just about to leave the capitol to catch a boat from
Albany for New York, but they assured Frances that they
would cast favorable votes before they left and that they
would instruct their political cronies from the Bowery to do
likewise. Big Tim and his cousin told the clerk of the senate
to record their "ayes," and instructed their cronies on how
to vote. Then they hurried away for the boat.

No sooner had the Sullivans left, however, when several
of Big Tim's Bowery cohorts changed their "ayes" to "noes."

Frances saw immediately that this trickery could easily result in the defeat of her bill. At this point young Franklin Roosevelt stepped into the breach. He told Frances to try and head off the Sullivans at the pier and get them to return. Meanwhile, he would lead a filibuster to delay the final vote.

Frances raced to a telephone and managed to intercept the Sullivans just before they boarded the boat.

"We'll be right back!" Big Tim roared.

The Sullivans leaped into a taxi, but the taxi stalled before they completed the return journey.

"We'll run the rest of the way!" Big Tim shouted at his cousin.

Which is what they did, arriving at the Legislature just a few moments before the doors were to be closed and locked for the night.

As soon as the King of the Bowery was back on the scene his cronies who had voted against the bill in his absence quickly switched their votes back to "ayes." At the end of the new roll call the fifty-four-hour work week bill awaited only the formality of the governor's signature to become a law.

Frances Perkins did not rest on her laurels following her first major triumph as a lobbyist. She began at once to intensify her campaign for industrial safety legislation. Largely due to her efforts, a legislative act creating a State Factory Investigating Commission was passed in 1912. Frances was named the director of the Commission, which immediately began a statewide survey of factory conditions. The findings of this survey shocked the public—just as the Triangle Fac-

tory fire had done. Charges were brought against the State
Department of Labor, and a number of bills for the pro-
tection of industrial workers were introduced into the State
Legislature.

For the next two years Frances and her colleagues fought
to persuade the Legislature to pass the safety measures,
which were called "The Thirty-two Bills." During these two
years the State House at Albany was locked in the most
stubborn struggle in its history. Manufacturers and real
estate owners whose buildings would have to be fireproofed
if the bills passed, brought tremendous pressures to bear
against the Legislature. Every political trick and maneuver
known was used to defeat the measures—but in the end they
were passed. And the reason they were passed was due to
Frances Perkins' calm, steady, well-reasoned, relentless presentation of facts and figures, the truth of which no one
could deny.

When Frances first appeared as an expert witness at a
hearing before the Factory Investigating Commission, a
lawyer hired to defend the real estate interests couldn't
believe his eyes.

"This little girl an expert!" he exclaimed.

But Frances soon proved to be a foe worthy of the experienced lawyer's mettle. She had no intention of making an
emotional appeal. She had hundreds of hard facts and
figures at her fingertips. They had been given to her by
completely unemotional men—safety engineers.

"And the wonderful thing about engineers," Miss Perkins
later said, "is that they don't know how to lie! Their whole
training and experience has to do with meeting natural laws,

not evading them. A lie won't bridge a river nor make a building safe. Engineers get in the habit of thinking and telling the truth and people recognize it in them."

In addition to safety engineers, Frances Perkins had also gained the support of corporations that were actively engaged in fire protection work. They helped her convince the legislators that adequate safety measures were not merely a matter of protecting the welfare of workers. There was also an extremely practical side to the matter. This was a fact that all successful manufacturers recognize today: the highest degree of safety for workers is actually the best profit-making policy; the elimination of accidents actually increases production.

Finally, all of "The Thirty-two Bills" were passed. One of the most important bills was a safety measure designed to protect people working in buildings more than three stories high from tragic disasters—disasters such as the Triangle fire.

4

LOVE AND MARRIAGE

Washington Place, where the Triangle Factory fire occurred, was not far from the apartment where Frances Perkins lived in a section of the city called Greenwich Village. Frances had lived in the Village since first coming to New York, a fact that caused her conservative New England parents some concern.

Greenwich Village was just becoming known as the gay, Bohemian, artists' center of New York City. Here young painters and writers and musicians and actors and actresses lived and worked and played together, sharing each other's stories and experiences of early success and failure. While the Village was not yet as famous as it would become in the 1920's, it already had about it much of the Parisian Left Bank artists' atmosphere—an atmosphere of which Frances' parents did not wholly approve.

Frances did not let their attitude influence her, however. "The main reason so many of us young people live here," she pointed out in her practical way, "is because it's a low-rent district, the lowest in the city."

In letters to her parents Frances often wrote about her new friends in Greenwich Village. This set her mother's and father's minds somewhat at ease.

Two of Frances' best Village friends were Mary and Charles Beard. They were destined to become widely known historians, but their famous book, *A History of the United States*, would not be published until 1921. When Frances first became acquainted with the Beards, she shared with them a common interest in welfare work. Charles Beard was one of the founders of the New School for Social Research in New York City, and he later directed the Training School for Public Service.

Frances also became acquainted with another young man who was to gain even greater fame as a writer. This tall, gangling, homely youth had graduated from Yale University in 1907 and then had come into New York to try his hand at free-lance writing. When Frances first knew him he regarded himself as a failure as a writer. Within the space of a few short years, however, his rise to success and fame was to be meteoric. In 1914 and 1915 his first two books, *Our Mr. Wrenn* and *The Trail of the Hawk*, would be published. They would be followed in the 1920's and 1930's by several satirical novels that would revolutionize American fiction. Among these books would be *Main Street, Babbitt, Arrowsmith, Elmer Gantry,* and *Dodsworth.* The young man was, of course, Sinclair Lewis, who was destined to win the Nobel prize for literature in 1930.

The name of another young man, Paul Caldwell Wilson,

also began to appear frequently in Frances' letters. Frances'
parents had all but decided that social work was to remain
their daughter's one and only love. When she had been
living at home with them in New England, they had encouraged her to become interested in any one of a number of
suitors, but she had chosen welfare work instead. Now it
appeared that she had just been waiting for the right young
man.

Paul Wilson was neither a writer nor a welfare worker
but a financial statistician. He was, however, active on the
political scene as the secretary to New York City's recently
elected reform mayor, John Purroy Mitchell, and this gave
him and Frances a strong bond of common interest. Frances
also found that Paul Wilson had a keen analytical mind
that was a great aid to her in helping her solve some of the
knotty problems she faced as a woman lobbyist struggling
to get her safety and industrial reform measures through
the State Legislature.

These early years in Greenwich Village proved to be the
happiest in Frances Perkins' life—and 1913 was the happiest
year of all. She had scored her first major successes as a
woman lobbyist at Albany, and she and Paul Wilson were
married.

After her marriage Frances—at her husband's insistence—
continued in her role as the secretary of New York's Committee on Safety and worked closely with the State Factory
Investigating Commission. She and her husband also agreed
that Frances should continue to use her maiden name in
her professional work.

"This was as a convenience to him," Frances later explained. "I didn't want Paul to be annoyed or embarrassed by my public service or political activities." If she had not been in public service work, she declared she would have insisted upon being known as Mrs. Paul C. Wilson.

The only cloud on the horizon during the early years of Frances and Paul Wilson's marriage was the same cloud that darkened the world's horizon—this was the First World War that began in Europe in the summer of 1914. In 1916, the year before the United States entered the conflict, the Wilsons' daughter—she was to be their only child—was born. Christened Susanna Winslow Perkins Wilson, the baby proved to be a delight to her mother and father.

With America at war Frances Perkins soon added to her myriad activities all kinds of additional social work. She acted as coordinator and director of all of New York's social service agencies. Later she was one of the founders of the Maternity Center, an organization that was responsible for the public health movement for expectant mothers. Finally, she acted as director of the Council on Immigrant Education.

Shortly after World War I, the newly elected governor of New York, Alfred E. Smith, asked her if she would serve as a member of the State Industrial Commission. (Governor Al Smith's brown derby hat was as well known as Frances Perkins' tricorne.) Before accepting the appointment, she talked it over with her husband. She was mainly concerned about how the job would affect the rich personal life that she and Paul and their baby daughter, Susanna, shared. Accepting the job would mean many absences from home on trips throughout the state. And when she was home there would be heavy brief cases filled with work that must be

Frances Perkins when she was named head of the New York State Labor Department

done in the evenings. Paul urged her to accept the job as a challenge, for a challenge it was since it would mark the first time in the state's history that a woman had served in this key role.

Frances Perkins proved to be so successful as a member of the State Industrial Commission that in 1926 Governor Smith named her the chairman of the State Industrial Board. In this position—and later as the state's commissioner of labor—she proceeded to make New York's Department of Labor a model of efficiency and productivity that many other states copied.

One of her great interests as the head of the Department of Labor of the leading industrial state in the nation was unemployment. She developed a system for the accurate reporting of employment trends in 1,800 New York factories that was an excellent barometer of employment conditions throughout the country. It soon became accepted as being more reliable than unemployment statistics issued by the United States Department of Labor.

Also during her period in the state's Department of Labor Frances Perkins was successful in getting her fifty-four-hour work week law changed to a forty-eight-hour law, limiting the working hours for women and children to eight hours a day, or forty-eight hours a week.

In 1928, a new governor was elected in New York State. Before turning over the reins of the state's government to his successor, Al Smith said, "There's one person you'd better get to know around here. She's a woman. Her name is Frances Perkins. She's able, and she's conscientious, and if you want a bit of advice, I'd say you'd better try and hang on to her."

The new governor smiled a broad, infectious smile—a smile that was one day to become famous throughout the world. He needed no such advice about Frances Perkins. The new governor was one of Frances Perkins' old allies from the legislative wars at Albany. His name was Franklin Delano Roosevelt.

5

BACK FROM THE BRINK

The Franklin D. Roosevelt who was elected governor of New York in 1928 bore very little resemblance to the young New York State senator with whom Frances Perkins had first become acquainted in 1910. In fact he seemed to Frances like a completely different person—both mentally and physically.

Mentally, Franklin Roosevelt had grown tremendously in stature. Much of this growth, Frances suspected, was directly due to Roosevelt's close association with the highly idealistic President Woodrow Wilson during World War I. Where Roosevelt had once seemed almost indifferent about the common man's lot, he was now proud to be thought of as the "poor man's brother." He was also keenly interested in world affairs, whereas formerly his interest had not seemed to extend much beyond the borders of the Roosevelt family estate at Hyde Park.

Physically, the change was even more marked—but not

for the better. No longer was Franklin Roosevelt the athletic young man capable of standing on his feet for long periods of time to lead a filibuster—as he had done in behalf of Frances Perkins' fifty-four-hour work week bill. A crippling attack of infantile paralysis had left his lower legs almost completely paralyzed.

Frances Perkins knew that it was something of a minor miracle that Roosevelt had lived at all following his near fatal attack of polio. It was a major miracle, she thought, that he had fought his way back from the brink of political oblivion to the governorship of New York State. Much of the reason for this great display of courage, she knew, had to do with Franklin Roosevelt's family background and early training.

Franklin Delano Roosevelt had been born on January 30, 1882, at Hyde Park, New York. His father James was a prosperous railroad official and landowner. His mother Sara was a member of the wealthy Delano family who were importing merchants.

Although his parents were wealthy, young Franklin was not a spoiled boy. His mother and father insisted that he study hard, work hard and play hard but that he behave himself and respect his elders at all times. He remained at home and was taught by tutors until he was fourteen. Many of his summers were spent at Campobello, a rocky Canadian island off the coast of Maine.

At the age of fourteen, Franklin entered Groton where he was a good student, managed the baseball team and was a member of the debating team. After graduating from Groton he attended Harvard, where he also made good grades and edited the student newspaper, the *Crimson*. He belonged to eight Harvard clubs but was unsuccessful in his attempt to make the varsity rowing crew.

After his graduation from Harvard University, Franklin entered the Columbia Law School in New York City. While he was still studying law, he and Anna Eleanor Roosevelt were married on March 17, 1905. Eleanor and Franklin were distant cousins, and they were also both related to Theodore Roosevelt, who was then President of the United States. It was "Teddy" Roosevelt who inspired in young Franklin his first interest in politics.

Franklin did not complete law school but passed his bar examination in 1907. He then joined a New York City law firm and soon began to take an active part in politics. Despite the fact that Hyde Park, the district in which Franklin and his wife lived, was a Republican stronghold, he decided to run for New York State senator on the Democratic ticket in 1910. To everyone's surprise he scored a substantial victory.

At Albany young F.D.R., as he was now called, became the leader of a group of young Democrats who were fighting against the same political machine that was being besieged by the young woman lobbyist, Frances Perkins. This political machine was called Tammany Hall. Following young F.D.R.'s successful filibuster to save Frances Perkins' fifty-four-hour work week bill, the party bosses began to sit up and take notice of this young senator from Hyde Park who didn't seem to be in the least afraid of Tammany Hall. In 1912, F.D.R. was elected to a second term in the State Senate, tallying a larger majority than he had two years earlier.

That same year F.D.R. was a delegate to the Democratic National Convention. He strongly supported the nomination for President a man who had become his idol, Woodrow Wilson. When Wilson was nominated and then elected, the new President called F.D.R. to Washington as assistant secretary of the Navy. He served in that post from 1913 to 1920.

When World War I began, F.D.R. worked tirelessly to ready the United States Navy for the conflict. When America entered the war, F.D.R. played a key role in breaking the back of Germany's submarine warfare. He did so by urging the construction of a fleet of submarine chasers and by suggesting a novel method of blocking off the North Sea to the German U-boats (Undersea-boats) by laying down a barrage of mines in the area. The subchasers and the belt of mines, plus the use of the convoy method by the American and British navies, ended the U-boat threat.

After the war, Roosevelt joined Woodrow Wilson's crusading efforts to get the United States to join the League of Nations, which was dedicated to ending war for all time. When both Wilson's crusade and his health failed, F.D.R. took up the torch from the faltering President's hands. He was one of the leading Democrats who insisted that the party continue to fight for America's entry into the League. As a result, F.D.R. was nominated for vice-president and James M. Cox, Governor of Ohio, was nominated for President on the Democratic ticket in the election of 1920.

But the American people were tired of wartime restraints and disillusioned about the results of Wilson's "war to end all wars." The Republicans, led by Warren G. Harding, who campaigned for a "return to normalcy," defeated Cox and

Roosevelt by the biggest margin in the nation's history up to that time. Roosevelt even failed to carry Hyde Park.

After this disastrous defeat, F.D.R. returned to private life to lick his wounds and practice law to support his family.

In the summer of 1921, the Roosevelt family was vacationing at Campobello Island, where F.D.R. spent much of his time sailing. One day he took his daughter Anna and two of his sons, Elliott and James, out with him in the family sailboat. While they were sailing they spotted a forest fire on a nearby island. Immediately they went ashore and helped put out the blaze. This took several hours. Afterwards, to cool off, they all went swimming.

In bed that night, F.D.R. suffered a chill followed by severe pain. The next day he had a fever, and a doctor was called. F.D.R. was ordered to remain in bed. The next day his legs were paralyzed. Within three days he was completely paralyzed from the chest down. He had been stricken with the dread poliomyelitis, or infantile paralysis, which had spread throughout the nation that summer.

There now began a grim fight to save F.D.R.'s life, a fight that lasted several weeks. When it was finally over, F.D.R.'s life was saved, but he was almost a complete cripple. He was not a helpless cripple, however. This he set out to prove almost as soon as he was allowed out of bed.

He still had the full use of the upper parts of his body, and he discovered that when he went swimming, the water's buoyancy enabled him to move about quite freely. He determined to swim as much as possible and to practice crawling to strengthen his arms. This he did for hours at a time, and soon his body above his waist became as strong as an athlete's, although his lower legs remained shriveled and virtually useless. In time he became such a powerful swimmer that people seeing him in the water could not believe he was a polio victim. Out of the water he had to wear heavy leg braces and be supported by friendly hands or use canes in order to stand and walk. But even when he was being wheeled about in a wheelchair F.D.R. gave an impression of such physical strength and energy that few people ever thought of him as a cripple.

By the mid-1920's, Roosevelt was again practicing law in New York City and had recovered from his illness sufficiently to be able to nominate New York Governor Alfred E. Smith for President at the Democratic Convention. Smith was not the party's choice that year, but Roosevelt again nominated him in 1928, and this time Smith was picked as the Democratic standard bearer. Smith then persuaded Roosevelt to run for the New York State governorship. After much debate F.D.R. finally agreed.

In the elections that fall Presidential candidate Al Smith was soundly defeated by Herbert Hoover, but F.D.R.—much to everybody's surprise—was elected governor of New York by a comfortable majority. Roosevelt was to serve in that post until he became President of the United States in 1933. One of Governor Roosevelt's most able aides and closest allies was Frances Perkins, who was the industrial commissioner for New York State from 1929 to 1933.

6

BOOM AND BUST

As New York's industrial commissioner, Frances Perkins was the labor head of a state that had between three and four million workers. This amounted to one out of every nine wage earners and one out of every eight factory workers in the entire country. She herself directed a departmental staff of some 1,800 employees.

From her vantage point as the head of the largest State Department of Labor in the forty-eight United States, Frances Perkins had a unique opportunity to become familiar with economic conditions throughout the nation. The picture she saw upon taking office early in 1929 appeared to be one of almost unparalleled prosperity.

A serious but brief postwar depression in 1921 had prevented the nation from returning to the economic "normalcy" promised by President Warren Harding. But when Harding died in office in 1923 and was succeeded by his vice-president, Calvin Coolidge, a period of booming economic pros-

49

perity followed. This "Coolidge prosperity" resulted in "Silent Cal's" being returned to office as President in the election of 1924.

Coolidge firmly believed in few, if any, government controls on American business and industry. This "hands-off" policy met with much favor among the people who were tired of wartime government controls and restrictions. "The business of America is business," Coolidge declared as he loosened the reins on all areas of the nation's economy. His words were like sparks that set fire to a wild, free-spending era the like of which the nation had never seen.

The relaxation of wartime restraints created a revolution in manners, morals and people's spending habits. This revolution resulted in the period's being called "The Roaring Twenties" or "The Jazz Age" (after the popular style of music of the times). Dancing was very popular, particularly one dance called "The Charleston."

The decade also brought greater freedom and independence for women. Women were now able to vote, following the passage of the Nineteenth Amendment, and for the first time they began to take part in many activities alongside men. They also began to express their newborn independence in other ways. Having traditionally worn their hair long, they now cut it short in "boyish bobs." Dresses which had been ankle-length were shortened. In all walks of life in this period of frantic postwar prosperity, an attitude of gay, reckless freedom seemed abroad in the land.

Frances Perkins applauded some of these changes. Others she deplored. She was, of course, very much in favor of women having the right to vote. She was not in favor of the outlandish knee-length dresses worn by some of the young "flappers," as the girls were called. She herself continued to wear her severe, three-cornered hats and sedate, business-like suits. (A caustic and unfair critic was later to comment that her street clothes looked as if they had been designed by the United States Bureau of Standards.) Nor did she approve wholeheartedly of the change in people's spending habits, although she was pleased to see the common working-man at last able to enjoy some of the things he had never dreamed of owning when she had first started out as a social worker. She just hoped and prayed the dream world in which everyone now seemed to be living would not end in sudden disaster and despair.

For more people seemed to have more money than ever before—and they were more than eager to spend it. And if they didn't have the money today, they seemed to have faith in the fact that they would have it tomorrow, so they bought goods on the credit installment plan (or hire-purchase plan as it was called in Great Britain). All the money that was needed to purchase goods was a few dollars as down payment, and the balance of payments could be made in "easy" installments.

Credit installment buying was not a new thing in the world. Back in the nineteenth century European and American merchants had sold furniture and other household goods in this way. But the system had never taken hold as it did in the United States after the end of World War I when automobiles began to roll from assembly lines in great quantities and everyone wanted to own his own car. In the early 1920's seven million people owned automobiles. By 1927 this number had more than tripled. Financing these purchases on an installment basis had become big business virtually overnight, and Frances regarded this aspect of economic change with more than a little skepticism.

Her thrifty New England background as well as her training in economics helped Frances Perkins to recognize the dangers in wage earners, who were totally dependent upon weekly salaries, mortgaging too much of their future incomes. What if they should become unemployed next week, or the week after? And despite what appeared to be a permanent economic boom, Frances Perkins was well aware of a disturbing amount of unemployment. Information provided her by her New York Bureau of Labor Statistics indicated there were serious pockets of unemployment right within her own state. And across the nation she knew there were several millions of unemployed factory workers.

Her old friends from her Greenwich Village days scoffed at her worries. There had always been periods of industrial unemployment, they pointed out. It was a seasonal thing. Or perhaps it was a matter of technological change—new methods and machinery being introduced in factories that resulted in temporary layoffs.

Frances Perkins thought the trouble went deeper than that. As far back as she could remember there had been not merely temporary, but chronic, unemployment in certain industries. Just a few years earlier, in 1924, the Russell Sage Foundation had released the results of a survey disclosing that in some seventy cities in thirty-one states, during good years and bad, an average of ten to twelve percent of *all* American wage earners—literally millions of men and women—were *always* looking for jobs. That indicated, to her at least, that there was a fatal flaw somewhere in this rosy picture of prosperity.

But when she pointed out these findings, her friends simply shrugged their shoulders.

"We've always had a certain amount of permanent unemployment," they said, "and we always will have. Unemployment is always with us—like death and taxes."

Frances Perkins remained unconvinced, but she didn't press the point. She knew her friends did not want to be reminded of the dark side of the coin—if indeed there was one. All they cared to regard was the bright side, the side of the coin that reflected only unlimited prosperity.

"If you don't believe the times are good, Frances," they admonished her, "look at real estate. Or better yet, look at the stock market. Poor people are making money just buying and selling lots. And *everybody's* getting rich buying and selling stocks."

This was true, she had to admit. Property values had gone sky-high. And investing money in stocks—"playing the market"—had become a national get-rich-quick craze.

Every day the price of stocks rose higher and higher on the New York Stock Exchange. A person buying a stock one day almost always found on the following day that the stock was worth more than he had originally paid for it. Thus, many people who gambled in the stock market saw themselves making what seemed to be huge profits. Since most people who sold their stocks turned right around and bought more, much of the money they *seemed* to be making was never actually received. Their profits were "paper profits."

Many people also borrowed money to buy stocks "on margin." The upward spiral of the market looked as if it would never end, however, and everyone in America began to dream of becoming rich without having to work for the money.

Frances Perkins watched and wondered. What she saw continued to cause her to shake her head in disbelief. She could not rid herself of the certain knowledge—part of it a woman's uncanny intuition, the rest of it based on the figures supplied to her by her Department—that there were serious threats of economic disaster in this wildly spiraling prosperity.

Frances Perkins was not completely alone in her doubts and wonderings. Bernard M. Baruch, a famous financier and advisor to Presidents, began to sell all of his vast stock holdings in 1928. That same year Joseph P. Kennedy, father of future President John F. Kennedy, decided to convert all of his stocks to cash and not reinvest the money. Roger W. Babson warned in 1929, "Sooner or later a crash is coming. There may be a stampede of selling that will exceed anything the stock exchange has ever witnessed."

But these warnings went unheeded.

In March, 1929, Herbert Hoover took office as President. Like Coolidge, Hoover did not believe in government controls on business. Instead, he said, he believed in "rugged individualism" on the part of businessmen. He also said, "We are in sight of the day when poverty will be banished from this nation."

America was now at the peak of its business boom. Just seven months later the catastrophe that Frances Perkins had feared struck the nation.

In early September, 1929, the New York stock market hesitated in its dizzying upward climb. Instead of buying stocks, people had started to sell them. A tremor of fear ran through the New York Stock Exchange and fanned out across the nation.

But the feeling of fear soon passed.

The market was just adjusting itself. There had been other periods of adjustment. They had been brief. This too would pass.

The next day the market again began to climb to new heights.

The nation breathed a collective sigh of relief.

Then came a gradual downward sag in the price of stocks that continued steadily through September and most of October.

And on October 24—"Black Thursday," as it was later called—the fatal blow fell. The greatest wave of stock selling ever known deluged the stock market, drowning bankers, brokers and get-rich-quick investors alike. The era of "permaent prosperity" was over. In its stead dark panic and black depression soon spread across the land.

7

FRANCES PERKINS CHALLENGES PRESIDENT HOOVER

One winter morning early in 1930, Frances Perkins was walking along a New York City street when she saw a well-dressed, elderly woman lift the lid from a garbage can and rummage through the can's contents. What was the woman searching for? Frances wondered.

A few streets further along, she saw other well-dressed women doing the same thing. These women were carrying paper bags. From time to time the women would take things from the garbage cans and place them in their bags. The truth suddenly dawned on Frances Perkins. These women were searching for anything edible and were putting these scraps of food in the paper bags to take home to their families!

Frances Perkins knew that it was against the law for these women to be scavenging for food that might spread disease. But neither she nor the several policemen who were nearby had the heart to deprive these women of what was apparently their last source of food. She, like the policemen, turned her back on the scene. But it did not leave her mind. The next morning, at Albany, she told Governor Roosevelt about it.

"I wonder how people like that manage to keep from stealing food," she added.

"I've wondered the same thing," Governor Roosevelt said. "But according to police reports very little stealing of food has been going on."

"Maybe we're not getting the whole picture," she said.

"Maybe we're not—in more ways than one. President Hoover keeps insisting it's just a 'temporary economic slump' we're experiencing."

Frances Perkins' brown eyes began to flash angrily. "Temporary slump!" she exclaimed. "It's an economic crisis!"

Governor Roosevelt smiled. "Not according to his figures. He says prosperity is just around the corner."

"What figures? I haven't seen them."

"They're probably in your office now. I sent them along just this morning."

Without further comment, Frances Perkins went in search of the report, doubting its accuracy even before she saw it. How, she wondered, could anyone talk of temporary slumps when the signs of economic crisis were on every hand?

The stock market collapse of the previous autumn had not only wiped out many people's investments, but had also started a chain reaction throughout the nation that threatened a complete breakdown in the economy. Trade had fallen off as credit had tightened. People who did have cash had become afraid to spend it. Overstocked tradesmen and

manufacturers were forced to close down their businesses
or to discharge their workers. Thousands and thousands of
these discharged workers had been buying not only automobiles but also furniture, phonographs, washing machines,
vacuum cleaners, pianos, sewing machines, radios and electric refrigerators on the installment plan. When they could
no longer meet their "easy" payments, these goods were
taken away from them. This was exactly what Frances
Perkins had feared might happen, but she took no satisfaction in seeing her worst fears confirmed. She was not an
"I-told-you-so" kind of person.

Many people had also begun to lose their homes when
they could no longer meet their mortgage payments. The
building of new homes had completely stopped. In many
subdivisions all of the houses were for sale—and there were
no buyers. Rental properties also went begging, and people
began to double and triple up in small apartments as several
generations of families began to live together under one
roof.

The report Governor Roosevelt had mentioned was on
Frances Perkins' desk. She studied it carefully. In it President Hoover quoted Federal Department of Labor statistics
that indicated business was improving.

"How on earth can business be improving," she asked herself aloud, "if unemployment is increasing?"

She read further. But unemployment *wasn't* increasing—
or at least it wasn't according to the Federal Department of
Labor.

"Impossible," she muttered. Half in anger, half in grim
determination, she pushed President Hoover's report aside

and from a drawer in her desk took out the most recent report from her own State Bureau of Labor. She studied it over for a time. Then she rang for her secretary.

"I would like you to take this down and issue it to the newspapers," she said. She then dictated a brief but detailed statement.

When her secretary had left, she went to work on other pressing matters. She did not think about her statement to the press until she left her office that evening. Then she was startled to see her name emblazoned in newspaper headlines.

Her heart sank. She had had no idea her words would cause this kind of stir. She had expected the statement to be printed, if it were printed at all, on the inside of the newspapers, buried somewhere in the back pages. But here it was for all the world to see.

She bought a copy of one of the New York papers and hastily read the story. Her words had been reported accurately enough. All of what she had dictated that morning was there, word for word. In her statement she had simply quoted her regular monthly report—prepared by her Bureau of Labor Statistics—on employment trends. These were gathered directly, she had pointed out, from some two thousand New York factories. These figures, she had said, presented a full account of unemployment in New York State. Unemployment, according to her figures—and she would swear to their accuracy—was steadily rising and had been rising for the past several months. It was unlikely, she had continued, that the situation in other states was totally different from the situation in New York. In other words—and the

newspapers had added this interpretation—the New York
State Department of Labor was right, and the Federal
Department of Labor was wrong. The newspapers had then
gone one full step further. They said that the New York
Industrial Commissioner was challenging the President's
accuracy!

Frances Perkins had not cleared her statement with Governor Roosevelt. She hadn't thought it was necessary. Now
she knew she should have done so. Already there were
rumors that Governor Roosevelt might be the Democratic
candidate for President in the next election, and everyone
would think that Roosevelt was responsible for this story,
that he had meant it to be a challenge to President Hoover.

Frances Perkins knew Governor Roosevelt would be furi-
ous at her for letting him be subject to such charges, and
she felt he would have every right to be.

That night was a long one for her. She slept little. She
could hardly wait to get to her office the next day.

When the next day finally did arrive and she put through
her call to the Governor, her apology was greeted by Roosevelt's amused chuckle.

"Apologize!" he exclaimed. "For what? I say bully for
you." ("Bully" had been a favorite expression of Teddy
Roosevelt's, and FDR had adopted it.) "Certainly I read
your statement, and I think it was an excellent one. I'm not
only glad you made it. I say keep up the good work!"

8

THE DEPRESSION DEEPENS

Frances Perkins did keep up the good work in the dark months ahead. And she was backed by Governor Roosevelt every step of the way.

The monthly statement on employment trends issued by her State Department of Labor was soon used by the newspapers as a barometer of employment conditions throughout the country. It was not only issued several days before the Federal Employment Index of the United States Department of Labor, but it was also generally accepted as being more reliable. Newspaper editors pointed out that the Federal Department of Labor had been editing its statistics to support President Hoover's falsely optimistic statements.

This fact, however, gave Frances Perkins no real satisfaction.

"We're not just dealing with figures on pieces of paper," she told Governor Roosevelt. "We're dealing with human beings—men, women and children who are out of work and hungry."

Governor Roosevelt agreed. Already he was making plans for what might be done on a national scale if the right man were in the Presidency. With Frances Perkins' help he had presented several reform bills to the New York Legislature. These included legislation for old-age pensions, unemployment insurance and a shorter work week. The latter bill was based on the theory that if those who had jobs worked fewer hours, there would be additional employment for those men who were out of work.

In 1931 Governor Roosevelt sent Frances Perkins to England to study unemployment conditions there. He hoped that she would return with facts and figures to support his proposed unemployment compensation bill.

Great Britain had adopted a compulsory system of unemployment insurance in 1911. From this side of the Atlantic it appeared to be a logical answer to the problem of people who were out of work. But on the scene in England, Frances Perkins could see that the plan was not a good one. She soon returned to the United States and reported to Governor Roosevelt that in practice the British *dole*, as it was called, had developed into a system of charity donations to the poor. The reason for this was that as soon as workers had used up their short-term unemployment benefits, the British government had begun to give free allowances to everyone who was out of work.

"That's the quickest way to break a man's spirit," she told the Governor. "People want to work for their money."

Her observation, Franklin Roosevelt was forced to agree,

was all too true. Perhaps the worst thing about the depression, he thought, was the way it went on year after endless year. Men who had been ambitious, self-respecting workers could get along going without a job for a few weeks, or even for a few months. But when the months drifted into years, the spirit went out of them. And in early 1932 there were some men who had been out of work since 1929 and had stood in breadlines and gone from factory to factory only to see the eternal sign, "No Help Wanted," staring them in the face.

"What suggestions do you have to make?" F.D.R. asked Frances Perkins.

Instead of free handouts, what she proposed was to try and find jobs for people. To do this she directed the activities of the New York State Employment Service. This was a statewide clearinghouse for job seekers. She also created a division called "Junior Jobs," a placement service for boys and girls under seventeen. Through these employment agencies she managed to seek out what few jobs there were available. And for those who couldn't be placed in jobs, she suggested direct state or federal relief. She knew, however, that at best her efforts were stopgap measures.

As the depression deepened, some twelve million men were out of jobs throughout the nation. People continued to go hungry. Unemployed men sold apples on street corners. Everywhere people in the cities cultivated every spare inch of ground to grow vegetables for food. These were not the "Victory Gardens" of World War I, but the keep-us-from-starvation gardens of the depression. Beefsteak fell from sixty cents a pound to nineteen cents a pound—and few per-

Unemployed workers during the depression selling apples on the streets of New York to earn their daily bread

sons had the nineteen cents in their pockets. Pork was so cheap that farmers stopped bringing their hogs to market. The price of wheat and flour fell to all-time lows.

What was needed, Frances Perkins felt certain, was direct federal control that would institute a nationwide recovery program. Daily she became more and more convinced that such control and direction would never come from President Hoover. He took the position that aid to the unemployed was the responsibility of private charities.

When the depression had reached its depth and even the optimistic Frances Perkins was beginning to have moments of serious despair, she was suddenly given new hope. Governor Franklin D. Roosevelt was being urged by the Democratic party to run against Herbert Hoover for the Presidency in 1932. And what truly sent her spirits soaring was her certain knowledge that if the nomination were offered him, Governor Roosevelt would accept.

9

FIRST LADY OF THE CABINET

"I hate telephones, automobiles, airplanes and everything that makes noise," Frances Perkins once told a newspaper reporter. Then she added for good measure: "And that includes the radio. I refuse to own one."

But in the early summer of 1932 she broke her own long-standing rule about not listening to the radio. The Democratic party was holding its national convention in Chicago, and she simply had to know how the contest was going among the three men who were seeking the nomination for President. She had a radio installed in the bedroom of her New York City home and listened to every session of the convention.

Two of the candidates were her long-time friends. They were the ex-governor of New York, Al Smith, and the present governor of New York, Franklin D. Roosevelt. The third candidate was John Nance Garner of Texas. Though she did not know Garner, she had heard good reports about his work as speaker of the United States House of Representatives. She supposed she shouldn't have a favorite among these three highly capable men, but she did have. Her sympathies were all with Governor Roosevelt.

On the first three ballots at the convention none of the three leading candidates had enough votes to be nominated, although Roosevelt had a commanding lead. Frances Perkins began to fear that the backers of the other candidates might combine their votes and defeat Governor Roosevelt. But just the opposite happened. James Farley, Roosevelt's shrewd political manager, reached an agreement by long-distance telephone with John Garner, who was in Washington. (It was not the custom for potential nominees to attend the nominating convention.) Garner released his backers so they could vote for F.D.R. On the fourth ballot Franklin Delano Roosevelt won the nomination for President. John Garner received the vice-presidential nomination.

Frances Perkins then overcame her distaste for the telephone and put in a congratulatory call to Franklin Roosevelt, who had remained at his governor's post in Albany. But the Governor was not available. He was in the process of doing two things that no other Presidential nominee had ever done before: first, he had chartered an airplane and was going to fly from Albany to the convention; and second, he planned to appear before the convention to make his acceptance speech in person.

Frances Perkins continued to remain close to the radio for most of the next twenty-four hours. She was listening the next night when Franklin Roosevelt made his dramatic acceptance speech in which he said, "I pledge myself to a

New Deal." Then he added, "This is more than a political campaign. It is a call to arms!"

That was the kind of challenge the depression-bound nation needed, she thought. And she knew that Franklin Roosevelt's campaign for the Presidency would also be bold and filled with the kind of challenge that the times demanded.

During the rest of the summer Roosevelt and Garner ran an extremely strenuous campaign against Herbert Hoover, who had been nominated by the Republicans for a second term as President, and Charles Curtis of Kansas, Hoover's vice-presidential running mate. Roosevelt's major speeches took him into thirty-eight states. Everywhere, he continued to pledge a "New Deal" for the American people. He also pledged himself to help "the forgotten man at the bottom of the economic pyramid. Above all," he insisted, "we must make bold experiments. With our nation in distress it is only common sense to try one plan, and if it fails, try another. The important thing is to try *something*. The millions who are in want will not stand idly by, forever silent, while the things to satisfy their needs are in easy reach."

Hoover also waged a vigorous battle, warning the people against Roosevelt's radical promises of federal action to combat the depression. Hoover said that if Roosevelt's plans were carried out, "Grass will grow in the streets of a hundred cities, a thousand towns."

But Frances Perkins sensed Hoover's fight was a futile one. She felt that the fall election would be a vote against the depression, and that meant a vote against Hoover, who had become the depression's symbol. And she was right. In

November Roosevelt polled over seven million more popular votes than Hoover. Roosevelt tallied 472 electoral votes
to Hoover's fifty-nine. Hoover carried only six states to Roosevelt's forty-two.

Shortly after Governor Roosevelt was elected the nation's
thirty-second President, Frances Perkins began to hear
rumors that she might be selected for a post in the federal
government. She paid little attention to these rumors until
one of her closest friends, Mary Dewson, confirmed them.
Mary Dewson had for many years also been a social worker.
Her most recent job, however, had been as head of the
women's division of the Democratic party—the female coun-
terpart of Roosevelt's manager, Jim Farley.

"It's true, Frances," Miss Dewson said. "F.D.R. is con-
sidering you for an important job in his administration."

What Frances Perkins did not know—and would not know
until years later—was that Miss Dewson herself had been
making every effort to clinch a federal job for her. For weeks
Miss Dewson had been urging her friends across the nation
to write letters and send telegrams to their local chambers
of commerce, fraternal lodges, women's clubs, university
presidents, local business and labor leaders and insist that
Frances Perkins be selected by F.D.R.

With a straight face Miss Dewson reported to her friend
that just the other day Governor Roosevelt had said, "You
know, Mary, it's really surprising how many people insist
that Frances Perkins work for me in Washington. You and
I have always thought a lot of her, but I had no idea of the
hold she has on the public mind."

After her talk with Mary Dewson, Frances Perkins was

well prepared with all of her arguments against a federal appointment, when Governor Roosevelt asked her to come and see him at the Roosevelt home on Sixty-fifth Street in New York City on an evening late in February, 1933.

When she arrived at the Roosevelt home, she was immediately shown up to the President-elect's study on the second floor. F.D.R. wasted no time in coming to the point.

"Frances," he said, "I've spent a lot of time thinking this over, and I've made up my mind. I want you to be my secretary of labor."

Frances Perkins remained silent for a moment. Then she said with great seriousness, "I thank you for the honor you pay me in offering me such a responsibility, but I don't honestly feel I am the right person for the job."

"Why not?"

"The main argument is that I'm not from the ranks of labor. I'm not truly a labor person. The labor movement in the United States has always had and will continue to expect to have a person from the workingman's ranks as secretary. Labor just will not be politically satisfied with an outsider."

"I disagree with you. I think the time has come for all working people, organized and unorganized, to have more than political consideration. You're certainly not holding back because you don't like the idea of being the first woman Cabinet member—the First Lady of the Cabinet, so to speak?" F.D.R. smiled at his own phrase.

"Not at all," she said, returning his smile. "I think it would be a good thing to have a woman in the Cabinet— if she's the best one for the job. It's just that I feel a woman secretary of labor should be a labor woman—from labor's ranks."

F.D.R. waved a scoffing hand. "Frances, I know your record in New York State, and I know you can accomplish the same things for the whole nation."

Frances Perkins decided to try another tack. "If I took the post I would want to do a great deal—many things you probably would not agree with."

"For instance?"

"Well, in broad terms I would make immediate proposals for federal aid to all of the states for direct relief to the unemployed. I would also insist on an extensive program of government-sponsored jobs—'made' work, you would probably call it—anything, to let all of the millions of idle men and women do some kind of an honest day's work for a day's pay. The pay would have to come from federal funds—at least to begin with."

"What else?"

"I would want some sort of federal law establishing minimum wages and maximum working hours. I would also want to abolish all child labor, and create a federal employment service similar to the New York State Employment Service. I would also want to set up a system of unemployment insurance—not like the British 'dole' but our own, unique American brand." Then she added her final thought. "Perhaps most important of all I would want to establish a plan for old-age insurance, a program that will give young workers a definite feeling of *security* when they look forward to their retirement."

When she had finished, she and Governor Roosevelt

both sat studying each other silently for several moments.

Finally F.D.R. said, "Frances, I agree with you one hundred and ten percent. More than ever now I want you to accept the appointment, so you can immediately begin to make plans to go ahead with your program. Agreed?"

"I agree," she said quietly.

As she left the study she glanced at her wrist watch. The discussion had lasted less than an hour.

10

THE NEW DEAL BEGINS

Saturday, March 4, 1933, was cold and cloudy in Washington. Today Franklin Delano Roosevelt was being inaugurated as the nation's thirty-second President, and Frances Perkins was to be sworn in as the first woman member of a President's Cabinet. (This was the last Presidential inauguration that would be held in March. Future inaugurals would be held in January.)

F.D.R. wore a heavy, fur-lined coat to protect himself against the chill. When someone commented about his wearing a coat with such a fancy fur collar in these poor times, Frances Perkins heard the President-elect say that the coat was a hand-me-down from his father.

She was dressed in her usual smart, if somewhat severe, business suit. She had a new three-cornered hat for the occasion. Her coat was of stout tweed. She and her husband, Paul, and their daughter, Susanna, attended the inaugural together. They sat on the platform in the company of Franklin Roosevelt's wife, Eleanor.

The inaugural ceremonies were held on the east side of the Capitol. A crowd of more than 100,000 wildly enthusiastic persons completely packed the huge Capitol square extending out from the east portico. Several hundred thousand more cheering spectators jammed the streets for the inaugural parade that was to follow.

When all of the dignitaries were in their places on the platform, Franklin Roosevelt walked down a ramp on the arm of his son, James. The ramp was covered with bright red carpeting. A sudden hush fell over the crowd as the ceremonies began.

Chief Justice Charles Evans Hughes administered the oath of office, and Franklin Roosevelt's voice rang out loud and clear as he repeated each phrase. Eleanor Roosevelt pointed out that Franklin's hand was resting on a Dutch Bible that had been in the Roosevelt family for generations.

The new President now moved closer to the microphones that would carry his inaugural address to millions of radio listeners throughout the land.

"President Hoover, Mr. Chief Justice, my friends," President Roosevelt began, and Frances Perkins was impressed —as she knew all of his audience must be impressed—by the strength and confidence in his voice.

"This is a day of national consecration," the President continued, "and I am certain that my fellow Americans expect that on my induction in the Presidency I will address them with the candor and decision which the present situation of the nation demands.

"This is a time to speak the truth—frankly and boldly. We do not need to shrink from honestly facing conditions in our country today. This great nation will endure as it has endured, will revive and prosper. So, let me first of all—"

He was interrupted by cheers.

"So let me first of all assert my firm belief that the only thing we have to fear is fear itself—nameless, unreasoning, unjustified terror which paralyzes needed efforts to convert retreat into advance."

The cheers began to drown out the President's words, but his voice rose resolutely, confidently, filled with ringing challenge.

"This nation asks for action, and action now. We must act and act quickly. It may be that an unprecedented demand and need for undelayed action may call for temporary departure from that normal balance of public procedure. If the occasion warrants, I will not hesitate to ask for broad executive power to wage a war against the emergency as great as the power that would be given to me if we were in fact invaded by a foreign foe."

The cheers were louder now, and as the President came to the close of his speech the cheering continued to grow in volume. "We do not distrust the future of essential democracy," he said. "The people of the United States have not failed. In their need they have registered a mandate that they want direct, vigorous action. They have asked for discipline and direction under leadership. They have made me the present instrument of their wishes."

The applause and cheers had become a roar, and Frances

Perkins shivered slightly. There was something a little terrifying in this animal-like voice of the crowd. She had noticed that the shouts of approval had been particularly strong when President Roosevelt spoke of making demands that would be similar to wartime powers. In Europe a mood like this had swept Fascist Dictator Benito Mussolini into power in Italy and Nazi Dictator Adolf Hitler into power in Germany. She was humbly grateful, and the nation could be humbly grateful, she thought, that this man who was now the leader of the most powerful country on earth was a good and God-fearing man whose basic plan of action was founded on his heartfelt conviction that the will of the people, not of a dictator, should be the law of the land.

Early that evening Frances Perkins and the other members of the Presidential Cabinet assembled at the White House to be sworn into office. Despite the fact that she was a woman, she was ranked last as a Cabinet officer. This had nothing to do with courtesy but was based purely on seniority. The Department of Labor had been established in 1913, making the secretary of labor the lowest ranking Cabinet officer.

As the new Labor Secretary looked about her she could not help but be impressed by the caliber of the other members of the Cabinet, and she wondered if in the trying days ahead she would measure up to their stature. First of all, there was Secretary of State Cordell Hull, a liberal from Tennessee who had served twenty-four years in the House of Representatives and two years in the Senate. Next was Secretary of the Treasury William H. Woodin,

President Franklin Delano Roosevelt's 1933 Cabinet. From left to right, F.D.R.; Secretary of the Treasury William Woodin; Attorney General Homer Cummings; Secretary of the Navy Claude Swanson; Secretary of Agriculture Henry Wallace; Secretary of Labor Frances Perkins, first lady of the Cabinet; Secretary of Commerce Daniel Roper; Secretary of the Interior Harold Ickes; Postmaster General James Farley; Secretary of War George Dern; Secretary of State Cordell Hull

an industrial tycoon who had been head of the American Car and Foundry Company since 1916. President Roosevelt had selected the governor of Utah, George H. Dern, as secretary of war, and the secretary of the Navy was Claude A. Swanson of Virginia, who had been chairman of the Senate Naval Affairs Committee in World War I when Roosevelt had been assistant secretary of the Navy. Daniel C. Roper, a skilled political leader from South Carolina, was secretary of commerce, and Homer S. Cummings, an able lawyer, was the attorney general. Another extremely capable lawyer, Thomas Walsh, had originally been named attorney general, but he had died of a heart attack just forty-eight hours before Roosevelt became President.

Rounding out the Cabinet were Postmaster General James A. Farley, Roosevelt's political manager; Secretary of the Interior Harold Ickes of Illinois, another lawyer and also a part-time politician who had backed F.D.R.'s uncle, Teddy, for the Presidency; Secretary of Agriculture Henry A. Wallace, an Iowa Republican who had been the editor of a farm newspaper and whose father had been the secretary of agriculture in the Harding-Coolidge Cabinet; and, finally, Frances Perkins herself.

Although she felt somewhat ill at ease and unsure of herself in the midst of these distinguished Cabinet members, all of them except Harold Ickes, Henry Wallace and Frances Perkins were to pass into virtual obscurity within the next decade.

Supreme Court Justice Benjamin Cardozo administered the oath of office to the Cabinet members, and as the Secretary of Labor swore "to support and defend the

Constitution of the United States," she interpreted the oath
to herself in her own way. To her the oath she was taking
meant that she was swearing that she would promote the
welfare of all wage earners within the framework of the
general welfare of *all* the people of the United States—a
framework in which no group should gain at the expense
of other groups. From long experience she knew that this
ideal—of all groups working for the good of the whole—
would be tremendously difficult to achieve. She knew that
there had been, and would be, many slip-ups along the
way, but she was also devoutly convinced that it was truly
an ideal that was well worth striving for. It was, in fact,
an ideal she had been striving for during most of her adult
life.

After the swearing-in ceremonies at the White House
Frances Perkins attended the inaugural ball with her husband and Susanna. She had been too busy in the days immediately before the inaugural to shop for a ball gown, but
her teen-aged daughter—who would soon be referred to as
a sub-deb in Washington society circles—had insisted that
her mother have a new gown. Usually Susanna was more
interested in her stubby-tailed Irish terrier, Balto, than she
was in social functions, but this time was different. Susanna
told her mother that she and one of her friends would go
on a shopping spree for the inaugural.

"Nothing too fancy now," her mother warned.

Susanna laughed. "Just don't you worry. It will be just as
you would order it—rather like the Rock of Gibraltar with
just a dash of style and a discreet touch of feminine appeal."

The dress had been precisely as ordered—black lace with

brilliants glittering around the décolletage—and Frances
Perkins was more than pleased to be able to wear it to the
ball. Susanna was also attractively dressed—in an accordion-
pleated dark voile with a wide, cherry-colored sash.

Almost before the ball had begun, however, the Secretary
of Labor received word from a White House messenger that
her presence was requested at the White House by the President. She was only able to remain long enough to hear
Metropolitan Opera Star, Rosa Ponselle, sing, "The Star
Spangled Banner." Leaving Susanna in Eleanor Roosevelt's
charge, she and her husband returned to the home they had
rented on Thirtieth Street. There she changed into her
"working clothes." Then she made her dutiful way to the
White House.

As she came up the long, curving walk, she saw that the
lights were burning in the President's study—lights that
would continue to burn night after long night as President
Roosevelt and his New Deal aides went into emergency
action to battle the economic crisis that gripped the nation.

11

THE FIRST HUNDRED DAYS

Frances Perkins had expected Franklin Roosevelt to waste
no time before going into action when he became President,
but she had no idea he would move as swiftly as he did.
When she arrived at the White House on the night of
March 4, 1933, F.D.R. and his aides were in the midst of
drafting his first Presidential proclamation for delivery to
the nation the following day!

The proclamation declared a "bank holiday" from Mon-
day, March 6, through Thursday, March 9. During this
period all banks throughout the United States would remain
closed to prevent the "panic withdrawal" of funds. The
proclamation also declared that the New York Stock
Exchange as well as stock exchanges in other cities would
be closed. On Thursday F.D.R. was calling the Congress
into an emergency session to deal in detail with the economic crisis.

When the Labor Secretary was told about the proclama-

Shortly after she became U.S. secretary of labor, Frances Perkins was presented with this plaque symbolizing, "Women's Emergence into the New Day"

tion, she asked, "Do you actually have the authority to declare such a nationwide bank holiday, Mr. President?"

F.D.R. grinned. "Yes," he said. "We've had to reach back a way for it, but in October, 1917, a Wartime Act was passed giving the President such authority. The Act was intended only for the emergency that existed then. Fortunately for us in this present emergency, the Act was never repealed."

Once again F.D.R.'s inaugural reference to wartime powers echoed in Frances Perkins' mind. He had meant the word quite literally, she now realized.

As if sensing her mild misgivings, F.D.R. said feelingly, "The people's money is in those banks, Frances. They *must* be saved."

The banking crisis that kept the lights burning in the White House as well as in the Treasury building and other administrative offices all that night had reached its peak almost at the very hour of President Roosevelt's inauguration. During the last several weeks of President Hoover's administration a nationwide banking panic had developed. It had begun in Michigan, where two major Detroit banks had been forced to close their doors following "runs" on them by customers demanding their savings. To stave off catastrophe the governor of Michigan had then temporarily closed all banks in the state.

Soon runs had started on banks in other states, forcing more and more governors to declare temporary bank holidays. The banking panic had spread steadily across the land until New York had closed its banks this very morning, Inauguration Day. This meant that banking throughout the nation was virtually suspended. Money in large sums was unobtainable. Checks were useless. Small coins had all but disappeared, since people were afraid that if they used their coins to make change they would have no money available to pay for small purchases. It had become more and more difficult for merchants to carry on their daily trade.

Frances Perkins accepted the fact that the government had to put its strength behind the banks and help prepare a program by which they could be guided safely through this disaster. She suspected, however, that some people would regard President Roosevelt's proclamation as a dictatorial economic move. But his reference to saving the nation's banks because the people's money was in them convinced her that the President was making this move as a humanitarian action.

When the Congress met in special emergency session on Thursday, March 9, Secretary of the Treasury Woodin had an emergency banking bill ready for its consideration. In the past such legislation had taken weeks, even months, to be passed. This bill was passed and on the President's desk for his signature within a few hours! It stated that all banks were to be placed under close government supervision, and only those that were in sound condition would be allowed to reopen. To strengthen these reopened banks their assets were to be backed by Federal Reserve notes.

Within a matter of days after this first piece of New Deal legislation was passed, people's confidence in banks began to return. By mid-March Secretary Woodin reported that some 1,500 banks were back in business and "panic runs" had ceased. F.D.R.'s aides were now preparing legislation that would enable the federal government to insure all savings accounts for their full amount up to $10,000, and when news of this reached the public, full confidence was restored almost overnight. Within a few more weeks almost 14,000 banks had reopened their doors, and the economic paralysis that had gripped the nation began to subside. By mid-May all of the nation's stock exchanges were allowed to reopen, and on its first day of business the New York Stock Exchange reported a sharp rise in stock prices.

But Frances Perkins, along with President Roosevelt and the rest of his New Deal aides, knew that surmounting this one crisis was merely the first faltering step along the way toward recovery. The national economy was still an extremely sick patient.

With the bank situation under control, the most pressing problem was relief for the nation's needy. F.D.R. held several meetings with his advisers to discuss this problem. They pointed out that it was an American tradition for relief to be handled by local community and state organizations—the same argument against federal relief that had been used by President Hoover.

"But relief funds have been exhausted by most states," the Labor Secretary pointed out.

Several other Cabinet members were afraid, however, that Congress would refuse to appropriate funds for the poor.

At this point Vice-President John Nance Garner spoke up. "Mr. President," he said in his Texas drawl, "when we came into office we promised the poor people that we would help them. I think it's just about time we got about doing it."

"Amen," Frances Perkins said.

Vice-President Garner's blunt statement, supported firmly by the Secretary of Labor, resulted in F.D.R.'s petitioning Congress for relief funds for distribution by the states. Within a matter of days Federal relief funds were made available.

Harry L. Hopkins was named administrator of Emergency Relief. Hopkins was a welfare worker from New York City, where he had been a close friend of both Frances Perkins and her husband, Paul Wilson, for many years. Hopkins, like Wilson, had served in the administration of New York's reform mayor, John Purroy Mitchell, before World War I. At the time he accepted President Roosevelt's appointment, Hopkins was chairman of the New York State Relief Administration. In time he was to become F.D.R.'s most trusted aide, making his home in the White House during much of World War II.

Although she had been one of the prime movers in obtaining federal funds for local relief, Frances Perkins knew this was at best a stopgap measure. As a more effective method of relieving unemployment and stimulating idle industry, she urged an extensive federal public works program. She believed that if such a program had been started in 1929 or 1930 the depression would never had been as bad as it was now. But it was better to start such a program now rather than not at all. Largely as a result of her urging, the Public Works Administration (P.W.A.) was established. The P.W.A. provided construction jobs on major dams and road-building projects that put money into the pockets of thousands of needy men.

As a result of the P.W.A. and other early New Deal

U.S. Representative Mary Norton of New Jersey and U.S. Secretary of Labor Frances Perkins discuss proposed labor legislation early in 1933

projects, Harry Hopkins reported in the fall of 1933 that there were one million fewer families on relief than there had been in March. Nevertheless, there were about three and a half million families still on relief in the fall of 1933. These families included almost sixteen million persons, about six million of whom were teen-agers.

To provide work for the men who were the heads of these families, Harry Hopkins later suggested the creation of the Works Progress Administration (W.P.A.). Not merely because of her friendship with Hopkins but because it had long been an idea she herself favored, the W.P.A. had Frances Perkins' wholehearted support. It provided a wide variety of federally paid jobs that were often supervised at the local level by trained social workers. Although in many instances the actual jobs consisted of "made" work, they nonetheless allowed people to keep their self-respect as they could not do on a "dole" system of relief. And maintaining one's self-respect had become a serious problem with many thousands of husbands and fathers who had been out of work and watching their families suffer since 1929.

Under the W.P.A., writers compiled state historical guides, artists painted murals on post office walls, laborers repaired public buildings and worked on town and city streets—all at the same rate of pay, a flat fifteen dollars a week. The fifteen dollars a week each man earned was scarcely a living wage, but it enabled many thousands of families to survive these desperate times.

Critics of the New Deal frequently scoffed at the W.P.A. workers as, "A bunch of leaf rakers." This particular criticism once caused the Labor Secretary to state sharply to a reporter, "The only W.P.A. leaf rakers I've seen have been men who were too old or too sick to do anything else. At that those old men had enough gumption to want to do *something* for their fifteen dollars rather than *nothing.*"

A regular rash of other New Deal agencies with alphabet names broke out during F.D.R.'s first few months in office. Among the most important were the Agricultural Adjustment Agency (A.A.A.), which worked for an increase in farm prices, and the National Recovery Administration (N.R.A.), which drew up trade codes of fair competition among businessmen. The Tennessee Valley Authority (T.V.A.) was a giant step toward developing the water resources of the Tennessee River drainage basin for the nation's welfare. Legislation proposing these agencies was approved with lightning speed. Bills submitted to Congress one day were frequently passed and back on President Roosevelt's desk the following day. During its 104-day session early in 1933—usually referred to as "The First Hundred Days"—Congress passed some sixteen pieces of major legislation, a record unequaled up to that time.

Among the earliest of these New Deal projects was one for which Frances Perkins was primarily responsible, and one of which she was always extremely proud. This was the Civilian Conservation Corps (C.C.C.)—a somewhat revolutionary program designed to put unemployed boys to work.

12

MADAME PERKINS AND THE C.C.C.

"Just let me tell you something," a reporter snapped at Frances Perkins. "The Labor Department is a Johnny-come-lately department in this government. The press can do a lot to help you. You can't do a thing to help the press." With those angry words the reporter strode out of the office, leaving behind a dismayed and somewhat bewildered Secretary of Labor.

What in the world did I do to cause that outburst? she asked herself. She began to think back over her actions during the few short weeks she had been in Washington. Since her first arrival she had expected to meet resentment from several quarters—but certainly not from newspapermen.

From the very beginning, for example, she had known that the labor movement would probably resent a woman's being named secretary of labor. William Green, president of the American Federation of Labor, had left little doubt about the fact.

"We will never be reconciled to her appointment," Green had said publicly when Franklin Roosevelt had named Frances Perkins to his Cabinet.

Already, however, the Labor Secretary had begun to make friendly overtures to Green and the members of his Federation, and she was certain she could win their support.

She had also suspected that her fellow Cabinet members might resent having a woman in their midst. Consequently, at the first official Cabinet meeting she had been determined not to speak unless spoken to. Toward the end of the meeting President Roosevelt went around the table asking questions of the officials and listened carefully to their replies. Finally he turned to Secretary Perkins and said, "Frances, you've been mighty quiet. Don't you want to say something?"

Frances Perkins did not want to say a word, but she knew she must. There was complete silence in the room, and all of the other Cabinet members were staring at her.

"When I was a child," she said finally, "my father used to rap his knuckles on the table and say, 'Fanny Cora, don't waste people's time with useless vaporings. If you have something to say, say it and stop. If you don't have anything to say, don't say it.' Right at the moment, Mr. President, I don't have anything to say."

An amused chuckle, which grew into general laughter, went around the table. Laughing louder than any of the others was President Roosevelt.

"Frances," he said, "I think you're going to be the best 'man' in the Cabinet."

That first brief flash of dry New England humor had

broken the ice. Since that day Secretary Perkins had not felt a moment's unease in the presence of her fellow Cabinet members, nor had they felt any with her.

But why was the press angry with her? And was it really the press—or just this one young reporter who had stomped out of her office so angrily? Come to think of it, he had been the *only* reporter who had tried to interview her today. Had she kept the others cooling their heels so often in her outer office that they had simply stopped trying to see her? If that was true—and she had an uneasy feeling that it was—she knew she had made a serious mistake. It was essential that the Labor Department's plans and activities be reported to the people of the nation, and that meant she simply had to have a good working relationship with the press. But why wasn't she getting along well with the reporters now? She always had at Albany and in New York City.

The answer was clear as day, she was suddenly forced to admit. The reporters were angry because she had been treating them shabbily.

She recalled that the newspapermen had begun to be irritated with her right after her first appearance in Congress late in March, when she testified in behalf of legislation for the Civilian Conservation Corps. Since it had been the first time she had come before a congressional committee as secretary of labor, she had been nervous and ill at ease. To conceal her nervousness, she had been very official in her manner, answering the congressmen's questions with what, she now realized, must have been an air of self-importance. How her father would have lit into her for that!

In her first congressional appearance as secretary of labor, Frances Perkins discusses plans for the Civilian Conservation Corps (C.C.C.) with U.S. representatives and senators

—*Wide World Photo*

After her appearance before the congressional committee, a dozen or more reporters had attempted to interview her, but she was too nervous to go through a second ordeal—a mass interview. She simply brushed on past most of the reporters. One of them, however, was able to stop her long enough to ask a question that caught her off guard.

"Miss Perkins," he said, "none of us have been told how to address you. As the first woman member of the Cabinet, that presents a problem."

"You may call me 'Madame Secretary,'" she said tartly, continuing hurriedly on her way.

The newspapers that evening reported only briefly on what the Secretary of Labor had said in her testimony in behalf of the C.C.C. Instead they concentrated on how she spoke. They used such words as "blunt," "brusk," "clipped," "sharp," "impatient." They went on to report fully the "imperious and regal manner" in which the Secretary of Labor insisted she be addressed as "Madame Secretary." Although Frances Perkins could not realize it at the time, she was to be known not only in Washington but throughout the land as "Madame Perkins" from that day on.

The day after her first appearance in Congress she had arrived at work to find her outer office filled with reporters. She knew she simply could not take the time to talk with them today. There was a small mountain of work awaiting her on her desk, and she had to prepare a detailed report for the President and Congress on exactly how the C.C.C. should operate if the legislation authorizing it were to be passed.

Again she brushed on past the reporters, this time without answering any questions at all.

Most of the newspapermen remained in her outer office for an hour or more, but then they left to cover other news sources.

Each morning for the next several days the reporters had continued to appear at the Labor Secretary's office, but gradually they had given up when she continued to refuse to see them, or put them off with brief, noncommittal answers. This morning there had been just the one reporter who had insisted on seeing her.

"Absolutely no interviews today, Miss Jay," she had told her secretary. (The secretary's name was Frances Jurkowiz, but she was always called "Miss Jay.")

When the young reporter had heard this refusal several times, he had burst into Frances Perkins' office, told her she needed the press—the press didn't need her, and stalked out.

An hour after the reporter had gone, Miss Jay, entering her employer's office, was surprised to find Miss Perkins not working but staring out the window.

"You know, Miss Jay," Frances Perkins said finally, "I think that I've been wrong, dead wrong, and that young man was right."

She immediately set about repairing the damage she had done. For the next several evenings she invited a few newspapermen to tea or dinner. Grudgingly each of them began to admit that "Madame Perkins" was not only a gracious hostess, but she was also an extremely nice person, and that the way she had been acting toward them seemed to be completely alien to her true self.

Then one morning in her outer office she stopped before a large group of reporters who had again gathered there.

"Gentlemen," she said, "I want to speak to you candidly.

As some of you may have gathered by now, I don't have much of a flair for public relations." Her smile was matched by a dozen wide grins. "It's difficult for me to be hail-fellow-well-met with reporters. I can't slap you on the back and say, 'Come on into the office, boys.' What's more I don't think I would if I could, because I just don't think of you as 'boys.' I've always found it pleasant and constructive to talk with newspapermen one at a time, but a mass interview terrifies me. I'm frank to admit, however, that I've been wrong in not understanding that when you reporters are sent to interview somebody you have to go back to your papers with news, that your jobs depend upon your getting that news."

There were nods and general words of approval.

Frances smiled broadly now.

"All right, boys, what do you want to ask me?"

A barrage of questions was immediately fired at "Madame Secretary." The questions came so thick and fast that she had difficulty understanding what the reporters were asking her. Finally she held up her hand.

"You see why I find this terrifying?" she said, smiling. "All right. It seems to me most of your questions have to do with the C.C.C. Why don't I just try and tell you the way President Roosevelt and I have worked it out up to now? Then you can ask me any questions you care to. But one question at a time—*please*!

"When the President and the Cabinet first got together to make plans for immediate work relief," she explained, "all of the emphasis was placed on providing jobs for *men* who were out of work. While I heartily approved these measures, I asked Mr. Roosevelt not to forget about the millions of *boys* and *young men* who were also out of work.

"I pointed out that a number of these youngsters have become migrants. They're riding freight trains from one part of the country to another in a desperate search for jobs. In fact my Department's Children's Bureau has already reported that several hundred thousand boys, and girls dressed as boys, are drifting around the country as hobos. It's a deplorable situation. The President agreed that it is.

" 'How do you propose to remedy the situation?' he asked me.

"I said I thought camps should be set up for unemployed boys and young men, camps where the boys can do such things as forestry work.

"Mr. Roosevelt again agreed. 'How do you think the boys can be selected and processed?' he asked me.

"That's what's been puzzling me, I said. I think the camps themselves could be staffed by Army men—but the training would not be military training.

"President Roosevelt reminded me that when he and I first talked about my taking the secretary of labor job, I mentioned wanting to establish a Federal Employment Service (called United States Employment Service in 1940) similar to the New York State Employment Service. 'Why not do that now,' he asked me, 'and have the Federal Employment Service process the men?'

"I told him I hadn't done anything about establishing such a service yet.

" 'Then establish it,' Mr. Roosevelt said.

"And that's just what I've been doing while you gentlemen

have been trying to see me. The Federal Employment Service is now ready to select and process boys for the C.C.C., just as soon as Congress passes the legislation."

As Frances paused in her explanation, the newpapermen immediately began to ask her questions.

"How much will each C.C.C. member be paid?"

"Each boy must come from a family on relief, and he will be paid a dollar a day for his work. All of the costs for his board, lodging, clothes, education and medical care will be met by the government. He will send all of what he earns except for twenty-five cents a week to his family, and the family relief allowance will be reduced by that amount."

"How do you think William Green is going to react to this plan?" another reporter asked.

"He's already reacted," Frances said wryly. "He was horrified by the idea of establishing a dollar a day as the wage for any work. I've tried to explain to him that this is relief money, not a wage scale. 'Just the same,' Mr. Green told me, 'the boys will be getting it as wages.' I told him it was just being *called* wages to save face, to give the boys a little pride in earning some money by the sweat of their brows. You men can help me get that point across to Congress and the public if you will."

Several reporters nodded their approval, indicating they would cooperate.

"How does the President feel about Mr. Green's reaction?"

"He's disappointed," Frances said. "He thought labor would be delighted with the C.C.C."

"Can you give us any more figures, any statistics on how many men will be involved?"

Miss Perkins started to speak, then stopped. She had already given up too much of her time in this interview, but she couldn't be too abrupt about bringing it to an end. She recalled how a little New England humor had saved the day at the first Cabinet meeting.

"Gentlemen," she said, "most of you know that I am a bug on statistics, but every once in a while I have to remind myself of my great-grandfather, Edmund Perkins. He lived to be well over one hundred years of age. On his one hundredth birthday he went to the local shoemaker and ordered the best pair of shoes that could be made. 'Mr. Perkins,' the shoemaker said, 'I don't see why you want to spend so much money for such a good pair of shoes. You don't honestly think you're going to live long enough to wear them out, do you?' To this my great-grandfather replied, 'There must be something wrong with your statistics. Don't you know that very few men die after one hundred?' "

Frances Perkins let the reporters' appreciative laughter die down. Then she said, "I really am sorry, but I must get to work now. And so must you."

The reporters dashed off to write their stories. Madame Perkins, they agreed, was really great "copy."

Before the end of the "First Hundred Days" of Franklin Roosevelt's New Deal administration the Civilian Conservation Corps was established. It proved to be one of the most successful of all of the New Deal efforts to bring relief to the depression-tossed nation.

Between 1933 and 1943, when the C.C.C. program was ended, some three million men were enrolled in some four thousand camps. These men planted two billion trees, built

The first C.C.C. unit goes to work near Luray, Virginia

more than 100,000 miles of roads and laid some 75,000 miles of telephone lines. They constructed six million small dams to control soil erosion. They also built numerous state parks and fought countless forest fires. C.C.C. enrollees also received training in many manual skills including truck driving and maintenance, welding, carpentry, plumbing and tractor and bulldozer operation.

The Labor Department's Employment Service selected and processed the men, Army officers and noncommissioned officers were in charge of them in the camps, and the Forestry Service supervised their daily work. When it began, the C.C.C. enlisted boys and young men in their teens. Later older men were admitted. So successful was the program that it led to several individual states establishing similar camps for dependent, delinquent or neglected young people.

In later years, after she had retired as secretary of labor, Frances Perkins was frequently stopped by men who would say to her, "You were a friend of F.D.R.'s. He must have been a great guy. I was in the Three C's, and it was the best experience I ever had in my life."

Even Army officers who at first objected to being placed in charge of civilians over whom they could exert no military authority, eventually gave their stamp of approval to the project. One of them once told Miss Perkins, "The Three C's gave me the greatest course in leadership I ever had. It taught me the importance of controlling and leading men by persuasion and example, rather than by iron-fisted authority. Later when we got into World War II and disciplinary problems came up, we had already learned how to solve them by persuasion and diplomacy."

But all of that was still in the future. Now there were still a number of serious problems that the Secretary of Labor had to face. One of the most serious of these problems had to do with winning William Green and the rest of the labor movement to her side, for despite Frances Perkins' optimism regarding her ability to deal with labor officials, there were serious threats of industrial warfare on the New Deal horizon.

Before industrial warfare actually broke out, however, she scored another important success. This was the sponsoring of legislation that would improve the welfare of the entire nation, an improvement that has continued right down to the present day. The project on which Frances Perkins went to work as soon as her C.C.C. bill was passed was called Social Security.

13

A SANE ANSWER TO
CRACKPOT PANACEAS

There was a contagious spirit of optimism abroad in the land as the early emergency measures of the New Deal began to take effect on the nation's economy. But there was still serious unemployment, and this caused many of the long-suffering poor to listen seriously to false prophets preaching crackpot panaceas to eliminate poverty. In a curious way these schemes were directly responsible for the passage of America's first Social Security Act.

In 1933 Upton Sinclair proposed a program on the West Coast which he called "End Poverty in California" (E.P.I.C.). Since California had a higher proportion of old people than other states, one feature of E.P.I.C. had an especially strong appeal. This was Sinclair's plan to give every unemployed person over sixty a monthly pension of fifty dollars.

Frances Perkins had followed Sinclair's career with considerable interest ever since she had first become seriously interested in social welfare work in Chicago. Sinclair's book,

The Jungle, published in 1906, had exposed the unbelievably
unsanitary conditions in Chicago's stockyards and meat-
packing industry. The book had shocked Miss Perkins—as
it had shocked the entire nation. In fact it had so aroused
public opinion that there was an investigation of the meat-
packing industry which resulted in the passage of federal
pure food laws.

Since then Sinclair had written a whole series of what
President Theodore Roosevelt had called "muckraking"
books, a term Roosevelt borrowed from Bunyan's *Pilgrim's
Progress*. In these books Sinclair continued to expose what
he saw as the evils of American industry. Frances Perkins
had applauded some of Sinclair's writing. Much of it, however, she thought was too radical and one-sided. When he
wrote on political subjects, she often found herself in violent
disagreement with him.

In 1926 Sinclair had run unsuccessfully for governor of
California on the Socialist ticket. In 1933 he was again plan-
ning on running for governor, this time as a Democrat, and
he believed that his program to end poverty in California
would get him elected. In addition to pensions for unemployed old people, E.P.I.C. included proposals to greatly
increase income and inheritance taxes, to tax idle land and
to establish a statewide system of cooperative business ven-
tures that would stimulate the economy. Sinclair lost the
election in 1934 by the narrowest of margins. After his defeat
E.P.I.C. collapsed.

Another California-based end-poverty movement was Dr.
Francis E. Townsend's, "Old Age Revolving Pensions." The
Townsend Plan proposed to pay all unemployed persons

over sixty years of age two hundred dollars a month. This money had to be spent within thirty days. Funds to support the Townsend Plan were to be obtained through a two percent transaction tax, that is, a national sales tax.

The Townsend Plan attracted a great many followers despite the fact that Frances Perkins and other responsible labor and fiscal leaders pointed out that if by some remote chance it did go into operation, half the national income would be required to take care of about nine million needy old people. Nevertheless the Townsendites and their curious crusade were a definite political force in the mid-1930's, attracting several million followers. In fact it was not until 1937 that the movement began to die.

There were numerous other end-poverty plans proposed during this period. (One was the somewhat cynical "Thirty Dollars Every Thursday" plan, which also promised free ham and eggs to all of its members.) But by far the most politically potent scheme was the "Share Our Wealth" program cooked up by the former cottonseed oil salesman and incumbent senator from Louisiana, Huey "Kingfish" Long.

The Share Our Wealth plan had an immediate appeal to the vast millions of unemployed since it was based on redistributing the nation's private fortunes. Senator Long offered his plan with several variations, but it always included the following basic points: all individual inheritances would be limited to five million dollars. Personal fortunes would be limited to eight million dollars. Maximum individual incomes would be confiscated by the government to be redistributed among the people in the form of a free house, automobile and radio to every family, plus an annual income of two

thousand dollars. Long also proposed a free college education
to all young people and pensions to the aged.

Although most economists laughed at the Share Our
Wealth program, millions of poor people across the nation
rallied to Huey Long's cause, and thousands of Share Our
Wealth clubs were formed. On the strength of such support Senator Long began to dream of becoming President.
His assassination on September 8, 1935, in a corridor of the
Louisiana state capitol building at Baton Rouge by a local
physician, Dr. Carl Austin Weiss, ended Long's dreams of
glory as well as the Share Our Wealth movement.

Both President Roosevelt and Frances Perkins believed
that the welfare of the nation's wage earners should be protected by unemployment and old-age insurance. The obsta-
cle that stood in the way of such insurance was America's
long tradition of self-reliance. Since pioneer days Americans
had taken a fierce pride in their ability to stand on their
own feet and not ask for financial assistance from their government. Now, however, the worst economic depression in
the nation's history had made most people modify this
independent attitude.

Young men realized that a desire to work did not neces-
sarily create jobs. Older men recognized the harsh truth
that they could suddenly lose their jobs and be face to face
with disastrous economic insecurity in their old age. It was
this climate of opinion that caused many people to become
interested in the various crackpot panaceas to eliminate
poverty and unemployment and to provide for the aged.
And it was this climate that made President Roosevelt and
Frances Perkins realize that the time was ripe for a sane
unemployment and old-age insurance proposal.

In June, 1934, F.D.R. appointed Miss Perkins as the head of a Committee on Economic Security.

"Everybody should be included in such a program," F.D.R. told her. "From the cradle to the grave every U. S. citizen should be covered by some sort of social insurance program. That's what I want you and your Committee to work out."

The executive director of her Committee was Professor Edwin Witte. The other members included Henry Morgenthau, Jr., Homer Cummings, Henry Wallace and Harry Hopkins. Arthur Altmeyer, assistant secretary of labor and later commissioner of Social Security, coordinated the work of the Committee and guided the bill through congressional hearings.

Frances Perkins went to work immediately to prepare legislation for presentation to Congress. Recalling her days in Albany when she had succeeded in getting bills passed by the New York State Legislature, she again used the technique of calling on experts for aid and advice. She called to Washington economists, statisticians, insurance executives —any and all professional men and women whose training and experience would prove valuable in preparing social insurance legislation and in convincing Congress of the need for such insurance.

She also received valuable assistance from a twenty-three-member Advisory Council appointed by President Roosevelt to represent labor, industry and the general public.

The deadline for presenting the legislation to Congress was early in 1935. As the deadline approached, she grew more and more fearful that the approval Congress had so far given almost all of the New Deal measures would now be withheld. The bill that was being prepared was, she knew, revolutionary. If it became a law it would be the first basic federal social welfare legislation in the history of the country.

F.D.R. was reassuring, however. "Frances," he said, "every man, woman and child in the country *has* to be guaranteed genuine security, a reasonable amount of leisure and a decent living throughout their lives. You know it, I know it, and I think you'll find that the Congress knows it."

Frances Perkins' fears were unfounded. Despite its revolutionary nature, the Social Security Act was passed by both Houses of Congress and placed on the President's desk for his signature by August, 1935. The legislation had been sponsored in Congress by one of F.D.R.'s and Miss Perkins' old friends from New York, Senator Robert Wagner. When President Roosevelt signed the bill, he called it, "The cornerstone in a structure which is being built but is by no means complete." He also paid glowing thanks to Frances Perkins and Senator Wagner for their efforts in behalf of the bill.

The Social Security Program, which began in 1935, was a blanket plan that offered protection to needy old people through pensions and public aid; it also promoted unemployment insurance throughout the nation and had provisions for the care of the blind, the care of dependent children and expanded the public health services. After the Act was passed Frances Perkins pointed out, "We would have had national health insurance too, but we couldn't get our data together in time." Health insurance on a nationwide scale was to come, of course, but not for more than thirty more years.

Social Security benefits have been expanded in many ways

Frances Perkins and other government officials at the ceremonial signing of the Social Security Act in President Roosevelt's office in the summer of 1935

since 1935. Almost immediately after the Act's passage, however, its benefits began to be felt. Before the passage of the bill less than five percent of the aged received payments from retirement funds. Most old people had to be supported by their families or by various charities. Today almost seventy-five percent of the aged population receives payments from social insurance and related benefits.

Among the changes later made in the Social Security Act was one that advanced the initial payment of monthly benefits from 1942 to 1940. A retired legal secretary, Miss Ida Fuller of Ludlow, Vermont, became the first old-age insurance beneficiary when she received Social Security check number 00-000-001 on January 31, 1940. In the next quarter of a century there would be more than twenty million beneficiaries.

Certainly one of the greatest strides forward accomplished by the Social Security Act was in aid to the unemployed. It helped establish a federal-state system of unemployment insurance. By offering certain tax benefits, it encouraged the individual states to set up systems of unemployment insurance along broad federal standards. Before the Social Security Act was passed, only Wisconsin had such an unemployment insurance law. Today all states have such laws.

There was an interesting bit of aftermath to the passage of America's Social Security Act in 1935. Great Britain, although regarded by many observers as far ahead of the United States in social welfare measures, did not adopt its broad social security program until December of 1942. It was called the Beveridge Plan, after Sir William Beveridge, its sponsor.

The Beveridge Plan was described throughout the English-speaking world as one that offered insurance coverage "from the cradle to the grave," a term that had first been used by President Roosevelt in talking with Frances Perkins. Beveridge had visited the United States in 1934 and talked at length with F.D.R. about social security. It was undoubtedly at this meeting that the British economist had picked up the "cradle-to-the-grave" phrase.

14

TROUBLES WITH LABOR

In 1936 Franklin D. Roosevelt was nominated for a second term as President. His running mate was again John Nance Garner. Their Republican opponents were Alfred M. Landon of Kansas and Frank Knox of Illinois.

A few days after his nomination F.D.R. talked with Frances Perkins about the coming campaign.

"Frances," the President said, "I want you to know that if I'm re-elected, you will continue to be my secretary of labor."

"In spite of all the trouble the labor movement has caused?"

F.D.R. waved a scoffing hand. "Growing pains," he said reassuringly. "Just growing pains. And you're the one who has to help them grow up."

Frances Perkins sat without speaking for a long time. There was no use blinking the fact, she told herself, that during most of President Roosevelt's first term in office there

112

William Green, president of the A.F. of L.; Frances Perkins, U.S. secretary of labor; and John L. Lewis, head of the C.I.O. and United Mine Workers

—*Wide World Photo*

had been serious trouble between industrial workers and
their employers. Try as she might, she could not rid herself
of the feeling that at least a part of the trouble was her
fault. And certain labor officials, she knew, would be the
first to agree with her. William Green was one. John L.
Lewis was another.

Should she resign as secretary of labor? she wondered.
Perhaps that would be the best way to solve the problem
of the industrial strikes that seemed to be plaguing the
nation. Despite her optimism when she had first taken
office, she had not had much success in gaining the support
of Green and his powerful American Federation of Labor
(A.F. of L.). She had had even less success in dealing with
Lewis and his Congress of Industrial Organizations (C.I.O.).

In a newspaper interview Lewis had said, "Madame
Perkins is woozy in the head. She doesn't know as much
about economics as a Hottentot."

At the time, the words had not made the Labor Secretary
angry. They had a certain rough humor about them that
she had appreciated. Recalling them now, however, filled
her with sudden angry determination.

"I'll show them who's woozy in the head," she said to
President Roosevelt.

F.D.R. looked blank for a moment. Then he threw back
his head and laughed his hearty, infectious laugh. He too
vividly recalled Lewis' sharp words.

"Bully for you, Frances!" the President said. "Bully for
you! We'll both show 'em."

Much of the controversy between labor and management
during F.D.R.'s first term had stemmed from two pieces of

New Deal legislation—the bill creating the National Recovery Administration (N.R.A.) in 1933 and the Wagner Act, which had been passed two years later.

One important section of the N.R.A. had given laborers the legal right to organize and bargain collectively with their employers over rates of pay, job conditions and so on. This greatly encouraged the growth of the labor movement. During the first year of N.R.A. more than a million workers joined the labor unions. When certain employers refused to recognize these unions, many employees refused to work. Strikes and violence over union recognition became widespread.

On May 27, 1935, the New Deal had suffered its first severe setback: the Supreme Court declared the N.R.A. unconstitutional. The administration had immediately sponsored a piece of labor legislation that would help fill the gap left by the defunct N.R.A. This was the National Labor Relations, or "Wagner" Act, so called because it was introduced by the same Senator Robert Wagner who had introduced the Social Security Act.

With the passage of the Wagner Act on July 5, 1935, workers no longer had to strike for union recognition and the right of collective bargaining. Unions continued to expand rapidly, union membership growing from about two and a half million in 1933 to some six million at the end of F.D.R.'s first term in office. But strikes continued. And they grew in size and violence as the unions grew. These strikes were held over wages and working conditions.

As secretary of labor, Frances Perkins had, of course, found herself right in the middle of all such difficulties. She had

The Secretary of Labor dons a steel helmet during an inspection tour

not always been too successful in solving the complex problems that had arisen between labor and management, but she had never failed to try and solve them. Not even threats against her life could prevent her from trying to do her job. And she had received several such threats in anonymous letters. She had taken the threats calmly, but F.D.R. had not. After she had received the first threatening letters, the President insisted that a detail of twenty-five policemen guard her at a dinner in Philadelphia where she spoke on labor problems.

As the 1936 election approached, she was more determined than ever to get labor and management to work together—that is, of course, if Franklin Roosevelt were returned to office.

On November 3, 1936, Franklin Roosevelt was re-elected President in a landslide victory. He carried forty-six states, Alfred Landon winning only in Maine and Vermont. Roosevelt received 523 electoral votes, Landon eight.

"I'd have got those other eight," F.D.R. told Frances jokingly, "if I'd have campaigned there!"

President Roosevelt's landslide victory did not end the administration's problems with strikes, however. In fact the year 1937 proved to be the most difficult of Frances Perkins' professional career.

First there was a series of "sit-down" strikes that spread from the rubber tire and automobile plants in Ohio and Michigan. The sit-down strike was a new technique adopted by workers who not only refused to work but also refused to leave the factories in which they were supposed to be working. Many responsible officials regarded the sit-down strike as illegal, claiming that the workers were unlawfully occupying property they did not own.

Frances Perkins was widely criticized when she commented, "There was a time when picketing was considered illegal, and before that strikes of any kind were illegal. The legality of the sit-down strike has yet to be determined."

Legal or illegal, the sit-down technique resulted in important concessions being granted workers in an Akron, Ohio, rubber plant. From there the fadlike sit-down movement spread to the Ford and General Motors plants in Detroit and then throughout the nation.

Also in 1937 there were threatened walkouts by laborers in the independent steel companies—Republic, Inland and Youngstown Sheet and Tube. As she had in other threatened strikes, Miss Perkins attempted to mediate between the workers and their employers. She visited the steel mills and personally talked with dozens of the workmen, many of whom were stripped to the waist in the blistering heat from the blast furnaces. The men were somewhat hesitant about talking to her at first, but she soon won them over by eating lunch with them in the workers' cafeteria and then matching pennies with one of the bosses to see who would pay the check.

During another attempt at mediation the Labor Secretary visited one of the steel mill towns to talk with anybody who wanted to talk with her. The local mayor, however, refused to let certain workers in to see her at the local town hall. Frances Perkins then adjourned the meeting in the town hall and tried to hold it in the town square. Again the mayor interfered. Miss Perkins was absolutely determined to talk with the workers.

The Secretary of Labor visits a textile mill

"Isn't there some private building we can use for our meeting?" she asked one of the workers.

At this point the local postmaster spoke up. "Why not use the post office, Madame Secretary?"

The Secretary of Labor looked down the street to where the postmaster was pointing and saw the American flag flying from the post office.

"It's a piece of federal property," the postmaster said, "and I don't think even the mayor would have the right to eject a federal official from it."

"You're right!" Frances Perkins agreed. She then marched down the street, leading her audience to the post office building and on inside, where under the Stars and Stripes she held her meeting.

When she returned to Washington, she called a press conference at which she said, "Espionage on the part of management, overspeeding, and irregularity of hours and employment are the sources of the major complaints that have come to me. Whether the complaints are justified or not, these are the unfair practices the working people are concerned with. . . ." She then added, "During my visit at the steel mills I also learned that a number of the workers earn only $500 a year—and a good many of them work seven days a week to earn that meager salary."

"Despite your visits to the mills it looks like the strike will still be held, Madame Secretary," a reporter said. "Do you have any suggestion for stopping all of the strikes the nation has been suffering from?"

"Yes," she said sharply. "It would be extremely helpful if Congress would pass legislation that would allow my Depart-

ment to issue subpoenas demanding the production of rec-
ords and the appearance of witnesses so we could inquire
into the true causes of industrial warfare."

When the interview with the Secretary of Labor appeared
on the front pages of the nation's newspapers, William Green
reacted quickly and angrily to the suggestion. "It would
only be a single step from compulsory attendance at Congressional hearings and the compulsory submission of testimony under oath to the compulsory acceptance of the
Labor Department's decisions. That would be compulsory
arbitration, and the A.F. of L. will have no part of Madame
Perkins' suggestions along that line."

It was following this disagreement with William Green
that Frances Perkins made up her mind to try and bring
the head of the A.F. of L. and the steel barons together so
they could work out some sort of mutual agreement that
would prevent a major steel strike. After a considerable
amount of effort she managed to get Green to meet with
the steel barons in her office in Washington. Among them
were the heads of the five major steel companies in the
United States as well as the executives of several smaller
companies. When they were all assembled in the Labor
Secretary's office, she was embarrassed to realize that most
of the steel barons did not want to talk with, or even to
meet, Mr. Green. They were apparently afraid that if they
met and talked with the president of the American Federation of Labor and this fact were reported in the newspapers,
the stockholders in their companies would accuse them of
collaborating with the enemy!

The Secretary of Labor was not only embarrassed for her-

The Secretary of Labor testifies before a congressional committee following one of her many inspection tours of industrial
plants

self but she was also embarrassed for Mr. Green. After this extremely difficult situation had continued for some minutes she became quite angry—she later described the situation as the "most embarrassing social experience of my life."

"Your behavior surprises me, gentlemen," she told the assembled steel barons. "I feel as though I had been entertaining a group of eleven-year-old children at their first party rather than the leaders of the most important industry in the United States!"

Sheepishly, the steel barons filed from the office.

It was because of such difficulties over mediation, however, that Miss Perkins finally decided to turn over many of the problems of her office to several of her assistants. The men she picked to bring peace to the strike-torn steel mills and auto industry were ideal selections for the job. They included Charles P. Taft, whose father, William Howard Taft, had been the twenty-seventh President of the United States; Lloyd Garrison, former chairman of the National Labor Relations Board; and Edward McGrady, the Labor Department's most accomplished trouble-shooter. All of these men had been schooled by Frances Perkins, and during the course of the next several years they managed to bring a certain degree of order out of the chaos that was the labor situation in the late 1930's. It was actually World War II, however, that resolved most of the nation's unemployment as well as labor-management problems.

15

AMERICA GOES TO WAR

When she had first come to Washington, few persons outside government circles recognized Frances Perkins when
they passed her on the street. In fact, one day in the mid-
1930's one of her old friends encountered her in a large
metropolitan department store. The friend was astounded to
see the Secretary of Labor walking alone and unnoticed
through the aisles.

The Secretary smiled at her friend's astonishment. "I'm
having a short holiday," she said, "and I must say I'm enjoy-
ing it tremendously. I can walk through this store, buy
whatever I wish, and nobody has the faintest idea who I
am. Can you imagine what a salesgirl's reaction would be
if she knew she were bargaining over prices with the secretary of labor?"

But Frances Perkins did not remain anonymous for long.
As the C.C.C., Social Security, N.R.A. and other New Deal
measures were written into history, her fame spread. During

the long weeks and months of the labor crisis her picture appeared in the newspapers almost daily.

For the most part, becoming a nationally known and nationally recognizable personality did not bother her. She didn't have time to be bothered. She was usually in her office from early morning until dinnertime. Several nights a week she returned to her office after a hasty meal to work until after midnight. Occasionally, however, she did find time to leave her exacting duties of endless study and consultations on labor problems. When she did, she sought complete escape.

One of the places where she was able to spend occasional quiet, private vacations was the Perkins' family homestead in New England. She was robbed of the pleasures of this hideaway when Mary Dewson, the friend who had helped her get selected as a member of the Cabinet, wrote a magazine article describing the Perkins' farm and the Labor Secretary's activities there.

"You've left me no place to hide!" Miss Perkins admonished Mary Dewson.

In the late 1930's and early 1940's she often spent week ends in Manhattan, staying with her daughter Susanna, who had recently married New York socialite David Meredith Hare. While these visits with her daughter and son-in-law were private, they seldom lasted very long, since she usually had to attend some dinner or other public function in the evenings. Consequently, when she really wanted to be alone on a weekend in Manhattan, she usually locked herself up in a room at her private club.

Frances Perkins' lovely daughter, Susanna, and Mrs. Franklin
Delano Roosevelt

On a Sunday afternoon in early December, 1941, Frances Perkins was in her private club room in New York when a telephone call came through to her from the White House switchboard in Washington from an operator called "Hacky," whom she knew well.

"The President has asked me to tell you there will be a Cabinet meeting tonight at eight o'clock," Hacky said.

"Tonight! But why? I'm working on a very special report."

But Hacky had hung up.

Fortunately, the Secretary of Labor was able to obtain a last-minute plane reservation. She quickly packed her few things and headed for the airport. There she encountered several other government officials who were also hurrying back to Washington. They seemed to know little more than she about the reason for the emergency Cabinet meeting. They had seen some banner headlines on some newspaper extras, but the headlines seemed impossible to believe.

As soon as they arrived in Washington, Frances Perkins went immediately to the White House. There she found most of the other members of the Cabinet in President Roosevelt's study. F.D.R. was not in his usual jovial mood. Instead, he seemed stern and icily calm as he spoke in a low hard voice to various military aides around him.

As soon as the entire Cabinet was assembled, President Roosevelt looked up from the papers on his desk and said, "All of you know what's happened. The actual attack began at one o'clock Washington time. I'm afraid we don't know many of the details yet. They're still coming in."

The Labor Secretary spoke up. "Mr. President, several of us have just arrived by plane. We haven't seen anything except some scare headlines. Could you tell us exactly what has happened?"

The President paused a moment. When he spoke, his voice was grim. "Why, yes," he said. "The Japanese have attacked Pearl Harbor."

At several earlier Cabinet meetings President Roosevelt had reported that a large Japanese Navy carrier force was at sea, but United States Naval Intelligence officers thought it was probably headed for Singapore. Army Intelligence officers, President Roosevelt had said, thought the Japanese fleet could be headed for the Philippines. No one had even mentioned the possibility of an attack against American warships anchored along battleship row at Pearl Harbor. Now, as the reports continued to filter into the President's study, everyone began to realize that the worst possible kind of calamity had befallen the American fleet. Slowly the knowledge also began to dawn on all of the Cabinet officers that although there had been no official declaration, the United States was now at war. As she sat and listened to the other members of the Cabinet ask the President questions about his immediate plans, the Secretary of Labor thought back to the time when she had first become aware of the possibility of America's entry into the war.

War clouds, she recalled, had darkened the horizon in Europe and the Far East as Franklin Roosevelt had begun his second term. In Spain there had been a bitter civil war. In Italy Dictator Benito Mussolini and his brown-shirted Fascists had completed their cruel conquest of Ethiopia and were threatening world peace. In Germany Adolf Hitler's black-shirted and brutal Nazis were also on the march.

President Roosevelt and his wartime Cabinet photographed at the White House just a few days after the Japanese attack on Pearl Harbor. From left to right around the table; Lend-Lease Administrator Harry Hopkins; Secretary of Labor Frances Perkins; Military Aide Colonel Philip B. Fleming; Vice-President Henry A. Wallace; Civil Defense Administrator Fiorello La-Guardia; Federal Security Administrator Paul V. McNutt; Secretary of Commerce Jesse Jones; Secretary of the Interior Harold Ickes; Postmaster General Frank C. Walker; Secretary of War Henry L. Stimson; Secretary of State Cordell Hull; President Roosevelt; Secretary of the Treasury Henry Morgenthau; Attorney General Francis Biddle; Secretary of the Navy Frank Knox; Secretary of Agriculture Claude Wickard

Italy and Germany had joined with Japan to form the Rome-Berlin-Tokyo Axis. Japan had been trying for years to conquer the whole of China and had begun to make threats against the United States and Great Britain. This had been the first real forewarning, she thought now. She also recalled President Roosevelt's telling her that the Axis powers were determined on a second world war, and it was up to the United States, Great Britain and France to stop them.

In trying to prepare the United States for the general conflict, President Roosevelt had met with much opposition from isolationist members of Congress who wanted America to remain neutral in case of war. In the face of this opposition, F.D.R. had done his best to build up the nation's defenses. When World War II was triggered by Germany's invasion of Poland in September, 1939, Roosevelt had kept the United States officially neutral for more than two years, but he had made it clear that America's sympathies were with Great Britain, France and ravished Poland. Gradually the American people had awakened to the fact that they simply could not remain calmly neutral with the worst war in the world's history raging around them.

During the period of official neutrality, the United States, at the President's urging, had agreed to a number of warlike measures. In addition to appropriating millions of additional dollars for national defense, a peacetime draft of men for the Armed Services was also adopted. Some munitions, certain kinds of war materials and fifty American destroyers were made available to the British.

In the midst of these efforts, F.D.R. had made another momentous decision. In 1940 he had decided to run for a third term as President, thus breaking the oldest rule in American politics. Many people, including the members of his own family, were opposed to his seeking re-election. Frances Perkins, however, backed him every step of the way, encouraging him to seek a third term and telling F.D.R. she would actively campaign for his re-election. She did this not because she was interested in continuing as a member of the Cabinet—actually she offered her resignation to F.D.R.—but because she felt the major work of the New Deal still remained to be done, and she was convinced it could only be completed by President Roosevelt. The tradition of the third term, she thought, was merely a tradition that could and should be broken.

F.D.R. was nominated by the Democrats on the first ballot at their national convention. His running mate was Henry A. Wallace of Iowa, former secretary of agriculture. Roosevelt's Republican opponent was a former Democrat, Wendell Willkie of Indiana. The Republican vice-presidential nominee was Charles L. McNary of Oregon. Although Willkie made it crystal clear that he was far from being an isolationist, he was nevertheless supported by those members of both parties who favored nonintervention as well as by regular Republicans. As a result, he gave F.D.R. more opposition than had Hoover or Landon. He polled forty-five percent of the popular vote but carried only ten states. F.D.R. tallied 449 electoral votes to Willkie's eighty-two.

As soon as he was re-elected, Roosevelt had returned to the task of preparing America for war. He was still strongly opposed by several isolationist senators, but despite their opposition F.D.R. managed to get Congress to pass the historic Lend-Lease Act in 1941. This Act enabled F.D.R. to "lease or lend war materials of all kinds to the Allied nations." It also allowed Allied warships to be repaired in the United States and encouraged the free exchange of military information between the United States and Great Britain.

The Lend-Lease Act, the Labor Secretary had known, was a step just short of war—and now, with the Japanese sneak attack on Pearl Harbor, the final step into war had been taken. Isolationist voices, she was certain, would immediately be stilled as a result of the Japanese attack, and all of the people would unite behind their Commander-in-Chief. Her job, she was also fully aware, would be more important than ever before. Not only would America have to train millions of fighting men, but these men would also have to be equipped with the weapons and materials for waging war on a global scale. "America," President Roosevelt had said, "must be the arsenal of democracy." Ahead, Frances Perkins knew, lay the greatest production demands in the nation's history. She hoped, and felt sure, that the labor movement would prove equal to the challenge.

16

THE WAR YEARS

America's entry into World War II was the final chapter in the history of the New Deal.

Until the war had begun in Europe the United States had continued to be plagued by serious unemployment despite the best efforts of President Roosevelt, Frances Perkins and the other leading New Dealers. In fact, as late as 1938 an economic recession had occurred that erased many of the employment gains made in the mid-1930's. When Hitler had invaded Poland in 1939 there were still some eight million unemployed workers in the United States. But as the fighting in Europe continued, war orders began to pour into American factories, and unemployment began to drop. Soon after the United States entered the war in 1941, unemployment was virtually eliminated. For the first time since the depression had begun in the early 1930's there were now more jobs than there were workers to fill them. No longer was fear of unemployment a specter stalking the land.

This rapid shift to full employment caused certain serious problems, however. For one thing workers continued to go on strike even when the nation's fighting men were risking their very lives to preserve the democracy that gave workers the right to strike. This caused a considerable amount of resentment on the part of servicemen manning America's far-flung battle lines.

Reasons for the strikes varied. Workers who had formerly been forced to put up with the worst kinds of working conditions now demanded better standards. As countless new war plants went into operation, they were staffed with inexperienced bosses who made mistakes in their methods of handling employees. The automobile and aircraft plants hired many young workers—many of them boys and girls who had dropped out of high school—and their lack of training and discipline was an invitation to disorder and hasty action. When strikes were threatened in such plants, Frances Perkins and her staff of Labor Department conciliators often could not get to the plants in time to head off the walkouts.

The C.I.O and A.F. of L. also continued their fierce drives for new union members. Some strikes resulted in plants where the new members of the labor movement demanded the right to organize.

As criticism of the labor movement grew both at home and on the fighting fronts, the Secretary of Labor urged President Roosevelt to call a White House conference of employers and labor leaders to try and iron out the difficulties. F.D.R. finally issued invitations to such a meeting. During the five-day White House conference that followed,

Frances Perkins on her sixtieth birthday

the industrial and labor leaders agreed to a pact that was in effect a labor-management truce. They agreed upon a "no-strike" pledge for the duration of the war. They also pledged to make a serious attempt to settle all disputes by negotiation and collective bargaining. Those disputes that could not be settled were to be turned over to a board appointed by President Roosevelt, and labor and management agreed to abide by the board's decisions.

This White House meeting and the War Labor Board that grew out of it solved most of the labor relations problems for the remainder of the war. There were still a few strikes, and some plants had to be seized by the federal government, but for the most part the labor movement and the nation's employers went to work with an iron determination to produce the tools of war that would defeat the Axis powers. This spirit matched that of the nation's servicemen who were fighting and dying in the greatest war the world had ever seen.

The output of steel and aluminum from United States plants increased in fantastic fashion. A synthetic rubber industry was created almost overnight to make up for the loss of natural rubber from Japanese-held Malaya and Indonesia. New war plants were built by the thousands. By 1943 more than half of the nation's industry had been converted to war production. Planes, tanks and trucks were manufactured by the automobile industry. Radar sets were produced by radio manufacturers. Vacuum cleaner plants made machine guns. Completely new shipbuilding methods were used to produce "Liberty" ships by the score.

The first year that America was in the war President

Roosevelt told his Secretary of Labor that the nation would have to produce 50,000 airplanes a year. For the first time in her life Frances Perkins felt fainthearted.

"We built less than a thousand planes last year," she told the President.

"The workers and manufacturers will find a way," F.D.R. said.

The President was right. Before the war ended planes were rolling off assembly lines at the rate of one every five minutes.

Total war was brought home to the American people as more than two million of the nation's women went to work in war plants. Frances Perkins indicated she had learned much about public relations methods when she referred to the typical American woman war-plant worker as "Rosie the Riveter." The phrase soon became a part of the common language of the wartime United States. Rosie the Riveter helped produce everything from an odd-looking little midget reconnaissance car that was to gain world fame as the Jeep, to the giant workhorse of a bomber, the B-24, both of which began coming from the assembly lines early in the war.

By 1942 American war production equalled that of the Axis powers. By the end of the war it was more than twice as great. For the Normandy invasion alone some 750,000 tons of supplies a month were shipped to England through 1943. This figure grew to almost two million tons a month by D-Day, June 6, 1944.

After the war the Labor Secretary often modestly pointed out that she had taken absolutely no part in actual plans for the conflict. She did sit in on all wartime Cabinet meetings, and in one extremely important way she and her Department played a vital wartime role.

President Roosevelt knew that the war on the home front could only be won by a complete team effort. This meant, first of all, that the heads of all government agencies must work together as a team. If there was bickering at the top, there would be little coordinated effort elsewhere in the nation. If there was complete cooperation among all government leaders, this spirit would be felt throughout the land.

At the same time, F.D.R. favored competition among various government agencies because a fierce competitive spirit could also start in Washington and from there spread like a blaze throughout the nation's war plants and fire the war workers to greater effort.

"You take over that job," F.D.R. told Frances Perkins. "Get 'em competing, but make 'em work together at the same time."

She accepted the challenge, as she had been accepting challenges all of her life. She became a member of virtually every interdepartmental committee in wartime Washington. The Department of Labor's offices became the meeting place for most of these committees. Here the Labor Secretary took the lead in alternately challenging committee members to greater effort and smoothing over ruffled feelings when the competition became too violent.

"By war's end," she later observed, "the Labor Department had as many meetings as the War Department. Sometimes I think people confused the two."

It was thus in the crucible of war that Frances Perkins

Two dear friends—Frances Perkins and F.D.R.

—*Wide World Photo*

truly mastered an art she had never quite mastered in peacetime—the art of mediation, of getting people to work together toward a common goal. Always afterward she credited President Roosevelt with inspiring her to this achievement, just as he inspired the rest of the nation to victory in World War II—a victory which, tragically, he was not destined to live and see.

17

DEATH OF A DEAR FRIEND

In 1944 Franklin Roosevelt decided to run for an unprecedented fourth term as President.

The end of the war in Europe now seemed in sight, but victory over Japan appeared at this time to be many months, if not years, away. Despite his obviously failing health, President Roosevelt felt it was his duty to remain in charge of the nation's fighting forces as Commander-in-Chief until final victory was achieved. He was also deeply involved in establishing a new world organization that would work toward permanent peace. This dream gradually was to become a reality as the United Nations.

If President Roosevelt were successful in his bid for re-election—and again she was certain that he would be—Frances Perkins was determined to resign from the Cabinet. She too had served an unprecedented length of time in office, and she was firmly convinced that a younger person should head the Labor Department, especially during the postwar period.

Roosevelt was renominated almost without opposition in the summer of 1944. His running mate was Harry S. Truman, a senator from Missouri who had done outstanding work during much of the war as head of the Committee Investigating the National Defense Program. The Truman Committee saved the government some fifteen billion dollars by helping to eliminate numerous cases of waste and mismanagement in war industries. Because of this, the Secretary of Labor was one of his strongest supporters. Roosevelt's and Truman's opponents were Thomas E. Dewey, governor of New York, and John W. Bricker, governor of Ohio.

From the standpoint of the popular vote the election proved to be remarkably close. In fact, before the final returns were in, several major daily newspapers heralded Dewey as the victor. When the final votes were counted, however, Roosevelt proved to be the winner in popular votes by 25,606,585 to Dewey's 22,014,745. In the electoral college the margin was much greater, Roosevelt garnering some 432 electoral votes to Dewey's ninety-nine.

Shortly before F.D.R. was inaugurated for his fourth term as President, Frances Perkins submitted her final resignation. It was ignored. Since the defeat of Germany seemed about to take place at any moment, she did not press the matter immediately. But shortly before Inauguration Day, she decided that she had to press F.D.R. into making a decision.

On the day before the inaugural, F.D.R. called a Cabinet meeting. This meeting was intended to be a mere formality,

Frances Perkins at the Democratic National Convention in July, 1944. It was at this convention that F.D.R. was nominated for a fourth term as President

—Wide World Photo

a gathering together of the members of the administration who had worked together as a family for the past twelve years. But the Labor Secretary could not let this opportune moment pass. She had told her staff that the day after F.D.R. was inaugurated to his fourth term in office there would be a new head of the Labor Department.

She had to steel herself to confront F.D.R. For one thing, he looked terribly tired, more tired than she had ever seen him before. His hands shook badly, his face seemed tight and drawn and his lips were pale and bloodless. He looked like a man driven far beyond the point of final endurance. Miss Perkins forced herself to bring up the subject of her resignation.

"Don't you think," she said, "I had better get Press Secretary Steve Early to announce my resignation today? I'll go in and write out the announcement."

"No," President Roosevelt said. "Frances, you can't go now. You mustn't force this on me. I just can't be bothered today. I can't think of anybody else, and I can't get used to anybody else. Not now! Do stay at your post and don't say anything. You're one hundred percent all right."

Then the President said something that Frances Perkins always thought of afterwards as their parting. He said it in a voice filled with exhaustion, and she knew that it was an effort for him to speak and that he was saying something that he deeply felt:

"Frances, you've really done awfully well, from the very beginning I mean. I know what you've been through, believe me. I also know what you've accomplished. I want to thank you."

President Roosevelt put his hand over her hand and gripped it. There were tears in the eyes of both. It was all the reward that his Secretary of Labor could have asked, her greatest reward since she had started out as a social worker in Jane Addams' Hull House and in the New York State Labor Department so very many years before. All she needed to know was that President Roosevelt had recognized the storms and trials she had faced in developing her Labor Department program, to know that she had been appreciated and that he was grateful.

After this meeting she saw F.D.R. only a few more times. A short time later he had a meeting with the other two Allied war leaders, Joseph Stalin and Winston Churchill, at Yalta. Shortly after he returned to the United States he addressed a joint session of Congress. He asked the assembled representatives and senators if he might sit down as he talked to them, the first time he had requested such a concession since he had been stricken with polio.

In the early spring of 1945 President Roosevelt decided to take a brief vacation at Warm Springs, Georgia. Since he had contracted infantile paralysis, the Warm Springs center had been such a favorite vacation and rehabilitation spot for F.D.R. that it was often called "The Little White House." On this particular trip he planned not only a short rest but also a work period during which he would sign official papers for the opening of the United Nations conference in San Francisco.

While he worked on these official papers, an artist also was busily at work painting F.D.R.'s portrait. In the midst of these activities, on the morning of April 12, 1945, President

Franklin Delano Roosevelt slumped over in his chair and died.

When she received the news in Washington about the death of her dear friend and colleague, the first thing Frances Perkins thought of was the fact that shortly before he left for Warm Springs Franklin Roosevelt had said to her, "The war in Europe is almost over, Frances. Now we must start working on the problems of peace."

She was deeply grateful that just a few short days before his death President Roosevelt had known that the end of the war was at hand.

18

THE LAST LEAF

In the early spring of 1953 a little old brown-haired lady—remarkably, her hair was unstreaked with gray—sat at her desk in a federal government office building in Washington, D.C. She was thinking back over the past several decades during which her life had been devoted to public service. Today, April 10, was her seventy-first birthday.

The tired yet indomitable little old lady in the tricorne hat was, of course, Frances Perkins.

She had been cleaning out her desk, for today at long last she was leaving Washington. Now she had paused for a moment, however, and was thinking back to how it had all begun for her. Just forty-two years ago—a span of years that would seem like more than a lifetime to most young people, but seemed like only a brief moment out of time to her—just forty-two years ago, there had been the Triangle Fire in New York City. That had been the tragic incident that had set her on the true course of her life.

147

Before that, of course, there had been the experience of Hull House and her sudden realization of the tremendous need of welfare work to be done in the world and of people like herself to do it. But actually it had been the Triangle Fire that had started it all. She also recalled her later experiences as head of the Labor Department in New York State and her growing friendship with Franklin Roosevelt. Where had the years gone, Frances Perkins wondered, the years that began back in some half-forgotten spring of her girlhood?

Her reverie was suddenly broken by Miss Jay's entering her office, followed by a man who looked vaguely familiar.

"Here's an old friend of yours," Miss Jay said.

"Yes, of course," Miss Perkins said, rising. She couldn't exactly place the gentleman, however.

"I had heard you were leaving, and I just wanted to stop in and say good-bye," the man said. "I see you've been packing."

"Yes, and I've not much to carry. Like a good soldier, I travel light."

The man laughed. "Can I help you?"

Frances Perkins sat down again behind her desk. "Yes," she said, "as a matter of fact you can. Would you mind packing up those last odds and ends?"

The odds and ends did not amount to much, she thought. Some thread, some needles, a prayer to St. Francis of Assisi, some badges from Democratic political conventions during President Roosevelt's administration. The letters from Franklin Roosevelt as well as those from President Harry Truman she would carry with her in her handbag. In her hand she held a final Presidential letter, one she had received just today. It was from President Dwight Eisenhower, wishing her well during her retirement.

Her visitor went eagerly to work. As she watched him packing her attaché case, the former Labor Secretary suddenly remembered this young man—or she remembered him when he had been a young man. He was young no longer. In fact, iron-gray streaked his hair.

"I remember you now," she said suddenly.

The man laughed. "Of course you do, Madame Secretary. I'm not surprised you didn't at first. I don't believe we've seen much of each other since you left the Labor Department."

Soon after Franklin Roosevelt's death, the resignation of the Secretary of Labor had been accepted by President Truman. He had not let her resign completely from government duties, however. He had insisted that she remain in Washington as a Civil Service commissioner. She had held this post for seven more years. On President Eisenhower's Inauguration Day she had submitted her final resignation, a resignation that "Ike" had reluctantly accepted.

"No, we haven't seen much of each other since then," she said. "But I remember you very well. You were the young reporter who told me off for not letting myself be interviewed by the newspapermen back in the thirties. I believe your exact words were, 'You need the press, the press doesn't need you.'"

The young-middle-aged reporter stopped in his work.

"Yes, Madame Secretary, I believe as a matter of cold fact that those were just about my exact words."

"I'm glad you said them," Frances Perkins said. "They brought me to my senses."

The reporter started to speak, stopped. Finally he said, "The fact of the matter is, Madame Secretary, I've come to revise that early estimate to a large degree. The blunt truth is I think not only the press but the whole country, all of us, needed you, and we've continued to need you. You haven't needed us at all."

Frances Perkins was silent for a time. Finally she said, "Well, thank you, young man. Thank you very much. That's about the nicest compliment—as a matter of fact it's one of the very few compliments I've had since I entered public life. It's particularly nice to have such a compliment paid to me on this day of all days, the day I'm bidding good-bye to Washington for good."

The reporter looked solemn. "You're the last of the New Dealers to go," he said quietly.

Miss Perkins' sense of humor suddenly seemed to reassert itself. "Yes," she said, "I'm the last tired leaf on the New Deal tree."

By now her attaché case was filled, and she rang for her secretary.

"I'm awfully sorry, Miss Jay," she said, "but I don't even know whether I've got enough money in my purse."

"You have," Miss Jay said. "I've checked just as always."

"Thank you," Frances Perkins said. She picked up her purse and attaché case and took a final look around the office. "The rest of my things will be sent on later I believe," she said.

Miss Jay nodded.

Frances Perkins as an elder stateswoman

"Can I give you a lift, or call a cab?" the reporter asked.

"Thank you. I would appreciate your calling a taxi."

As they walked down the corridor, the veteran government official said to the reporter, "You know, if you're going to do a story about my departure you might point out that I'm going to have to get my first Social Security card now that I'm leaving government service."

"You mean you don't have one yet?"

She shook her head. "President Roosevelt wanted me to take Social Security card number one as a special favor, but I refused. I told him that I had never believed in special privileges on the part of government officials, and I didn't see why I should start then. As a government official and as a Civil Service commissioner I never needed a card." Then she added with wry humor, "Now that I'm going to have to work for a living I guess I'd better get one."

When he had hailed a taxi and helped Miss Perkins into it, the reporter stood by the curb and watched it move slowly away. He waved in a manner that looked almost like a salute. The lady inside the cab returned his wave, but she did not look back. She sat primly in the back seat and, as she had done all of her life, looked straight ahead.

After her retirement from government office Frances Perkins made her home at New Castle, Maine. She did not remain idle, however. She was a visiting lecturer in labor relations and political science at the University of Illinois; a visiting lecturer for a seminar on American Subjects at Salzburg, Austria; a Regents Lecturer at the University of California at Los Angeles; and a lecturer at Cornell University. She also busied herself with writing a book to be called *The Al Smith I Knew.* (In 1946 she had published a book about F.D.R. called *The Roosevelt I Knew.*)

In her last years Frances Perkins was no longer regarded as a controversial person, as she had often been when she was United States secretary of labor. In fact she was generally accepted as an elder stateswoman whose opinions on labor problems were sought out by public officials.

In the spring of 1965 Frances took a short leave from her job as a lecturer at the New York State School of Industrial Relations at Cornell University for a routine physical examination. While in Manhattan's Midtown hospital she suffered a stroke. Several days later, on May 14, at 7:00 P.M., Frances Perkins died at the age of eighty-three. She was survived by her daughter Susanna (now Mrs. Calvert Coggeshall) and a grandson, Tommy. Her husband, Paul Caldwell Wilson, had died in 1952.

When news of Frances Perkins' death reached Washington, Secretary of Labor W. Willard Wirtz paid his predecessor a most fitting tribute.

"Every man and woman in America who works at a living wage, under safe conditions, for reasonable hours, or who is protected by unemployment insurance or Social Security is Frances Perkins' debtor."

BIBLIOGRAPHY

Allen, Frederick Lewis, *Since Yesterday* (Harper, 1940).

American Council on Public Affairs, *Federal Government Today: a Survey of Recent Innovations and Renovations* (The Council, 1938).

Babson, Roger W., *Washington and the Revolutionists* (Harper, 1934).

Bird, Caroline, *The Invisible Scar* (McKay, 1966).

Brogan, Denis W., *The Era of Franklin D. Roosevelt* (Yale, 1950).

Compton's Pictured Encyclopedia (F. E. Compton). Article on Franklin D. Roosevelt.

Current Biography: 1940 (H. W. Wilson). Biography of Frances Perkins.

Encyclopaedia Britannica. Articles on Franklin D. Roosevelt and Social Security.

Filler, Louis, ed., *The Anxious Years: America in the Nineteen Thirties* (Putnam, 1963).

Gillis, Adolph and Ketchum, Roland, *Our America* (Little, 1936).

Hurd, Charles, *When the NEW DEAL Was Young and Gay* (Hawthorn, 1965).

Kane, Joseph Nathan, *Facts About the Presidents* (H. W. Wilson, 1959.)

Kirkland, Winifred and Frances, *Girls Who Became Leaders* (Harper, 1932).

Leighton, Isabel, ed., *The Aspirin Age: 1919-1941* (Simon & Schuster, 1949).

Lord, Walter, *The Good Years: from 1900 to the First World War* (Harper, 1960).

Perkins, Frances, *People at Work* (Day, 1934).

Perkins, Frances, *The Roosevelt I Knew* (Viking, 1946).

Perkins, Frances and St. Sure, J. Paul, *Two Views of American Labor* (Institute of Industrial Relations, University of California, Los Angeles, 1965).

Sherwood, Robert E., *Roosevelt and Hopkins: an Intimate History* (Harper, 1948).

INDEX